THE CUTTING EDGE

Philosophy of the SAW Films

C. J. Patton

"Jigsaw" by C. J. Patton

U.S. Copyright Registration No. TXu 1-719-833
issued February 14, 2011

ISBN: 0615751806
ISBN-13: 9780615751801

To Mom and Dad.

CONTENTS

Chapter 1

INTRODUCTION

Most people who choose to see horror films do not watch them for philosophy instruction— far from it. And most mainstream horror films do not espouse philosophy beyond a simplistic and commonplace morality. But there are rare exceptions. When horror movies do more than shock, startle and scare—when they also convey life lessons reinforced by graphic imagery—they can teach and even transform people in a most potent manner. The *SAW* film series has that kind of power, and this may help explain why it is history's most successful horror film series.[1]

The *SAW* series consists of seven horror movies. One was released each year from 2004 to 2010. Based on original screenplays, the movies convey a unique morality that is grounded in an eclectic array of philosophical themes ranging from the ideas of Aristotle to those of Jean-Paul Sartre. The principal messages are that people should cherish their lives and the lives of others, determine yet accept their own identities, and grasp the significance of the will to survive. These philosophical teachings are imparted through the deeds

---

1   Guinness World Records. "Most Successful Horror Film Series." *guinnessworldrecords.com.* Guinness World Records. 25 July 2010. Web. 1 February 2013.

and pronouncements of the protagonist, John Kramer, a decent man and brilliant engineer transformed by tragic circumstances into a mad philosopher who seeks to enlighten others through torture.

Primary Messages

Many of Kramer's core beliefs about appreciating life, such as achieving happiness through moral action, pursuing true happiness rather than pleasure, and never justifying anything as a means to an end, are similar to the ideas of Aristotle.[2] Kramer's views that people can determine their own identities and that each person should accept his or her identity, yet never fear it changing are similar to Sartre's existentialist thinking.[3] Kramer's third primary message, that the will to survive is a key element of life, is comparable to Arthur Schopenhauer's view that the will is "fundamental to the universe."[4]

These messages were summarized well by Oren Koules, one of the producers of the *SAW* series, who said, "It was basically a message of . . . enjoy every day you live and respect the fact that you are able to live and do something with your life."[5]

---

2   Frost, S. E. *Basic Teachings of the Great Philosophers: a Survey of Their Basic Ideas.* New York: Anchor, 1989. Page 95. Print; Melchert, Norman. *The Great Conversation.* Fifth ed. 2 Vols. New York: Oxford UP, 2007. Page 186. Print.

3   Frost, S. E. *Basic Teachings of the Great Philosophers: a Survey of Their Basic Ideas.* New York: Anchor, 1989. Page 266. Print.

4   Frost, S. E. *Basic Teachings of the Great Philosophers: a Survey of Their Basic Ideas.* New York: Anchor, 1989. Page 96. Print.

5   *Hacking Away At SAW.* Prod. Mark Atkinson and Kelly L. Pancho. Lions Gate, 2005. DVD.

Plot Summary

John Kramer was the central character of the *SAW* movies. He was an engineer who worked on low-income housing projects, and he also helped his wife operate her health clinic.[6] He was a good man trying to help others who were less fortunate. Then Kramer's life was transformed by a series of traumatic events: his wife's miscarriage late in pregnancy, Kramer's diagnosis with terminal brain cancer, and Kramer's failed suicide attempt.[7] After these events, he still wanted to help people, but his methods became violent.

Faced with his own impending death from cancer, Kramer spent his remaining days attempting to enlighten others through torture.[8] He chose people whom he deemed criminal, unethical, or "unworthy of the life

---

6   *SAW IV*. Dir. Darren L. Bousman. Screenplay by Patrick Melton and Marcus Dunstan. Prod. Gregg Hoffman, Oren Koules, Mark Burg, James Wan, and Leigh Whannell. Perf. Tobin Bell, Scott Patterson, Luis Ferreiera. Lionsgate, 2008. DVD.

7   *SAW IV*. Dir. Darren L. Bousman. Screenplay by Patrick Melton and Marcus Dunstan. Prod. Gregg Hoffman, Oren Koules, Mark Burg, James Wan, and Leigh Whannell. Perf. Tobin Bell, Scott Patterson, Luis Ferreiera. Lionsgate, 2008. DVD; *SAW*. Dir. James Wan. Screenplay by Leigh Whannell. Prod. Gregg Hoffman, Oren Koules, and Mark Burg. Perf. Leigh Whannell, Carey Elwes, Danny Glover. Lionsgate, 2005. DVD.; *SAW II*. Dir. Darren L. Bousman. Screenplay by Leigh Whannell and Darren L. Bousman. Prod. Gregg Hoffman, Oren Koules, Mark Burg, and James Wan. Perf. Donnie Wahlberg, Beverley Mitchell, Franky G. Lionsgate, 2006. DVD.

8   *SAW II*. Dir. Darren L. Bousman. Screenplay by Leigh Whannell and Darren L. Bousman. Prod. Gregg Hoffman, Oren Koules, Mark Burg, and James Wan. Perf. Donnie Wahlberg, Beverley Mitchell, Franky G. Lionsgate, 2006. DVD.

they live," and put them in situations, called traps, where they had to fight for their lives.[9] Each trap was designed to teach a moral lesson that usually incorporated one or more of Kramer's three primary messages. Although Kramer believed that he never directly killed anyone, his traps were almost always life-threatening, gruesome, and very difficult to escape. Most traps resulted in people dying.

As Kramer's workload increased and his strength decreased, he needed help. He took on three accomplices, all of whom had survived traps. Kramer's three accomplices became very important characters throughout the series and are discussed in detail in the next chapter.

Once the media began sensationalizing Kramer's work, they started calling him the Jigsaw Killer. This is because Kramer cut a puzzle-shaped piece of skin from his test subjects.[10] As the number of traps grew and the theories about them became increasingly mysterious and confusing, some people began referring to the traps as the Jigsaw Case. After Kramer died, one of his accomplices was sometimes referred to as "the new Jigsaw Killer."

Test Subjects

Kramer preferred to refer to the people he trapped as his "patients" or "test subjects" rather than "victims."

---

9   All Traps are described in the Trap Index.
10 *SAW II*. Dir. Darren L. Bousman. Screenplay by Leigh Whannell and Darren L. Bousman. Prod. Gregg Hoffman, Oren Koules, Mark Burg, and James Wan. Perf. Donnie Wahlberg, Beverley Mitchell, Franky G. Lionsgate, 2006. DVD.

After Kramer trapped his doctor, he had this to say about him: "I was his patient and he was mine."[11] It is clear that Kramer did not believe that the victims of his traps were actually victims of anything except their own actions. Generally Kramer chose to trap masochists, con-artists, adulterers, liars, thieves, kidnappers, drug dealers, drug abusers, uncaring doctors, and murderers.

Traps

Kramer referred to his traps as "games" or "tests." A test subject would awaken in a trap and discover instructions usually starting with "I want to play a game," and ending with "Live or die—make your choice." These instructions almost always described how to escape or survive the trap and they often explained why the subject was put in the trap. After the instructions were given, the test subject sometimes found clearly labeled tools that would be needed to escape, or possibly a riddle to help them escape the trap. For example, one subject was told, "Sometimes you see more with your eyes shut," implying that the subject needed to turn off the light in order to see something written in glow-in-the-dark paint.[12] Failing a trap was often marked by the words, "game over." On one of the rare occasions when a subject succeeded,

---

11   *SAW III.* Dir. Darren L. Bousman. Screenplay by Leigh Whannell and Darren L. Bousman. Prod. Gregg Hoffman, Oren Koules, Mark Burg, and James Wan. Perf. Tobin Bell, Shawnee Smith, Angus MacFadyn. Lionsgate, 2007. DVD.

12   Trap Index, #10C; *SAW.* Dir. James Wan. Screenplay by Leigh Whannell. Prod. Gregg Hoffman, Oren Koules, and Mark Burg. Perf. Leigh Whannell, Carey Elwes, Danny Glover. Lionsgate, 2005. DVD.

Kramer's message was, "Congratulations—you are still alive—most people are so ungrateful to be alive—but not you—not anymore."[13]

Traps ranged from quite simple to highly complex in structure, but almost all were quite difficult to escape. In one simple trap, the subject was shackled at the ankle and could escape only by cutting off his foot.[14] Complex traps often required groups of people to work together in order to succeed. In one test, a group of criminals were locked in a house together, breathing in a deadly nerve gas. They could acquire an antidote from a safe, but they had to work together to solve a complicated riddle that would enable them to crack the code.[15]

Traps could be fraught with irony. The best example was a trap for a drunk who had repeatedly attempted suicide. To escape, the subject had to navigate through a maze full of razor wire, cutting himself to live rather than to die. The instructions concluded with one of the most frequently quoted lines of the *SAW* series: "How much blood will you shed to

---

13   Trap Index, #7; *SAW*. Dir. James Wan. Screenplay by Leigh Whannell. Prod. Gregg Hoffman, Oren Koules, and Mark Burg. Perf. Leigh Whannell, Carey Elwes, Danny Glover. Lionsgate, 2005. DVD.

14   Trap Index, #10B; *SAW*. Dir. James Wan. Screenplay by Leigh Whannell. Prod. Gregg Hoffman, Oren Koules, and Mark Burg. Perf. Leigh Whannell, Carey Elwes, Danny Glover. Lionsgate, 2005. DVD.

15   Trap Index, #11; *SAW II*. Dir. Darren L. Bousman. Screenplay by Leigh Whannell and Darren L. Bousman. Prod. Gregg Hoffman, Oren Koules, Mark Burg, and James Wan. Perf. Donnie Wahlberg, Beverley Mitchell, Franky G. Lionsgate, 2006. DVD.

stay alive?"[16] That question could be asked in many of Kramer's traps.

Potential test subjects often had the opportunity to avoid being trapped because Kramer provided advance warnings. Instead of simply kidnapping and putting subjects in a trap, Kramer would first hint that he was watching or considering them. This gave them a chance to correct their behavior before it was too late. For example, Kramer led the police to believe that an innocent doctor was the Jigsaw killer. This strategy made the doctor aware of Kramer's traps and allowed him to hear the testimony of a trap survivor. Kramer wanted the doctor to know that Kramer was targeting people that were like the doctor himself—people who didn't appreciate their lives.[17] Another example of a warning was when a detective went to inspect the corpse of one of Kramer's test subjects and saw words written on the ceiling telling him to "Look closer."[18] The detective then had the chance to reflect on why he was being called out and hopefully to reconsider his life.

---

16 Trap Index, #5; *SAW*. Dir. James Wan. Screenplay by Leigh Whannell. Prod. Gregg Hoffman, Oren Koules, and Mark Burg. Perf. Leigh Whannell, Carey Elwes, Danny Glover. Lionsgate, 2005. DVD.

17 *SAW*. Dir. James Wan. Screenplay by Leigh Whannell. Prod. Gregg Hoffman, Oren Koules, and Mark Burg. Perf. Leigh Whannell, Carey Elwes, Danny Glover. Lionsgate, 2005. DVD.

18 *SAW II*. Dir. Darren L. Bousman. Screenplay by Leigh Whannell and Darren L. Bousman. Prod. Gregg Hoffman, Oren Koules, Mark Burg, and James Wan. Perf. Donnie Wahlberg, Beverley Mitchell, Franky G. Lionsgate, 2006. DVD.

The prototypical trap of the *SAW* series was the Reverse Bear Trap, which was used three times. [19] The first time the trap was used, the subject awoke with a device around her head that was hooked into her upper and lower jaws. "Think of it like a reverse bear trap," Kramer said in the instruction tape. The subject needed to remove the device in less than 60 seconds. Her instructions conveyed that she could retrieve the key that would unlock her device if she cut open the stomach of her dead cellmate. Although she discovered that her cellmate was alive, she nevertheless cut him open to get the key, and was able to unlock the device in the nick of time. Had she not, the device would have permanently ripped open her jaw. [20]

All of these traps were intended to help people change their lives for the better. However, most of the traps were brutally violent and the only way to escape was to survive. Because of this, most test subjects failed, and even if they succeeded, their lives did not

---

19   Trap Index #7, #25 and #29; *SAW*. Dir. James Wan. Screenplay by Leigh Whannell. Prod. Gregg Hoffman, Oren Koules, and Mark Burg. Perf. Leigh Whannell, Carey Elwes, Danny Glover. Lionsgate, 2005. DVD.; *SAW VI*. Dir. Kevin Greutert. Screenplay by Patrick Melton and Marcus Dunstan. Prod. Gregg Hoffman, Oren Koules, Mark Burg, James Wan, and Leigh Whannell. Perf. Tobin Bell, Costas Mandylor, Mark Rolston. Lions Gate, 2010. DVD.; *SAW: The Final Chapter*. Dir. Kevin Greutert. Screenplay by Patrick Melton and Marcus Dunstan. Prod. Gregg Hoffman, Oren Koules, Mark Burg, James Wan, and Leigh Whannell. Perf. Tobin Bell, Costas Mandylor, Besty Russell. Lions Gate, 2010.

20   *SAW*. Dir. James Wan. Screenplay by Leigh Whannell. Prod. Gregg Hoffman, Oren Koules, and Mark Burg. Perf. Leigh Whannell, Carey Elwes, Danny Glover. Lionsgate, 2005. DVD.

substantially improve.[21] Kramer's violent traps were perhaps a reflection of the terrible car crash that marked the final step of his transformation and reinforced his appreciation of life.[22] Unfortunately, despite Kramer's intentions, the brutality of his tests was not able to restore the same appreciation for life in most of his test subjects.

---

21 See Detective Hoffman's follow up with Simone (Trap Index #23) in *SAW VI* for an example of this.

22 *SAW II*. Dir. Darren L. Bousman. Screenplay by Leigh Whannell and Darren L. Bousman. Prod. Gregg Hoffman, Oren Koules, Mark Burg, and James Wan. Perf. Donnie Wahlberg, Beverley Mitchell, Franky G. Lionsgate, 2006. DVD.

Chapter 2:

FEEL WHAT HE FEELS[23]

Kramer went through a profound emotional transformation before he started trying to enlighten people through his traps. To understand Kramer's lessons, one must analyze the emotional process he went through. Tobin Bell, the actor who played Kramer, described his character as follows: "He wants them to know what it feels like to have to struggle for your own life—people who sometimes see other people struggling, see patients struggling for their lives, but don't necessarily have as much compassion as

---

23 The body of this book has been organized into three chapters. "Chapter II: Feel What He Feels" describes Kramer's life, the events that caused his transformation, and how he lived afterward. "Chapter III: See What He Sees" explores Kramer's philosophical framework and compares it with the views of famous philosophers. "Chapter IV: Save as he Saves" provides a detailed philosophical analysis of the three primary messages of the movies. The concluding chapter discusses the morality of Kramer's methods and the justification for conveying lessons about morality via horror movies. These Chapter Titles are named after the three main traps in *SAW IV*, the middle movie of the series. *SAW IV* focused on a series of interwoven traps called "See What I See," "Feel What I Feel," and "Save as I Save," which Kramer designed and implemented to help everyone understand his point of view. Trap Index, #20.

they might."[24] Part of what Kramer wanted to accomplish with his work was to teach others to feel what he felt.

Pre-Transformation

Before the tragic events in his life, Kramer ran an organization called the Urban Renewal Group. Kramer was a skilled engineer whose job was to design buildings to house low-income families.[25] Kramer was very interested in helping others. He used his talents and abilities to do what he could for those who could not do better for themselves. Most people would have considered him a decent man.

Kramer valued happiness over pleasure. A concrete example of this is when a prostitute solicited Kramer on the night his transformation began.[26] "What are you doing? Do you know what this building is? It's a health clinic. You're a beautiful girl. Go home," Kramer said to her.[27] This illustrates that he valued his happiness over

---

24 *Hacking Away At SAW*. Prod. Mark Atkinson and Kelly L. Pancho. Lions Gate, 2005. DVD.

25 *SAW IV*. Dir. Darren L. Bousman. Screenplay by Patrick Melton and Marcus Dunstan. Prod. Gregg Hoffman, Oren Koules, Mark Burg, James Wan, and Leigh Whannell. Perf. Tobin Bell, Scott Patterson, Luis Ferreiera. Lionsgate, 2008. DVD.

26 Trap Index, #11, Test Subject #8; *SAW II*. Dir. Darren L. Bousman. Screenplay by Leigh Whannell and Darren L. Bousman. Prod. Gregg Hoffman, Oren Koules, Mark Burg, and James Wan. Perf. Donnie Wahlberg, Beverley Mitchell, Franky G. Lionsgate, 2006. DVD.

27 *SAW IV*. Dir. Darren L. Bousman. Screenplay by Patrick Melton and Marcus Dunstan. Prod. Gregg Hoffman, Oren Koules, Mark Burg, James Wan, and Leigh Whannell. Perf. Tobin Bell, Scott Patterson, Luis Ferreiera. Lionsgate, 2008. DVD.

pleasure because his long-term relationship with his wife was far more important than a night with a prostitute.

Transformation

Kramer's wife had a traumatic miscarriage after seven months of pregnancy due to an accident at her place of work.[28] This was the night Kramer's transformation started. This is when he began feeling that life is unfair—bad things happen to good people, and good things happen to bad people. It did not matter how ethical and kind he had been. The tragedies in his life just seemed to happen, and there was no accounting for them.

While Kramer was in the hospital with his wife just after her miscarriage, there was a specific scene that marked the beginning of his transformation. His wife was lying on a hospital bed holding Kramer's hand, when she said to him, "All I wanted to do was help them," referring to the addicts she treated at the health clinic. To this Kramer said, "You can't help them. They have to help themselves." He suddenly let go of her hand, stood up, and threw his watch in the trash.[29] Ironically or perhaps paradoxically, Kramer would soon

---

28 *SAW IV*. Dir. Darren L. Bousman. Screenplay by Patrick Melton and Marcus Dunstan. Prod. Gregg Hoffman, Oren Koules, Mark Burg, James Wan, and Leigh Whannell. Perf. Tobin Bell, Scott Patterson, Luis Ferreiera. Lionsgate, 2008. DVD.

29 *SAW IV*. Dir. Darren L. Bousman. Screenplay by Patrick Melton and Marcus Dunstan. Prod. Gregg Hoffman, Oren Koules, Mark Burg, James Wan, and Leigh Whannell. Perf. Tobin Bell, Scott Patterson, Luis Ferreiera. Lionsgate, 2008. DVD.

proceed down a path of trying to help people help themselves.

Kramer's misery and frustration became much worse after he was diagnosed with a frontal lobe tumor.[30] He consulted a surgeon, who determined that the tumor was malignant and inoperable.[31] Kramer sought experimental treatment, but was denied coverage by his health insurance company.[32] He became hopeless and anti-social, pushing everyone out of his life and rejecting all of his blessings. This devastating sequence of events drove Kramer to attempt suicide by driving his car off a cliff. Amazingly, he survived the crash, and that unexpected outcome completed his transformation.[33]

Post-Transformation

Even before his suicide attempt, Kramer believed that "once you see death up close, then you know what the

---

30 *SAW.* Dir. James Wan. Screenplay by Leigh Whannell. Prod. Gregg Hoffman, Oren Koules, and Mark Burg. Perf. Leigh Whannell, Carey Elwes, Danny Glover. Lionsgate, 2005. DVD.

31 *SAW III.* Dir. Darren L. Bousman. Screenplay by Leigh Whannell and Darren L. Bousman. Prod. Gregg Hoffman, Oren Koules, Mark Burg, and James Wan. Perf. Tobin Bell, Shawnee Smith, Angus MacFadyn. Lionsgate, 2007. DVD.

32 *SAW VI.* Dir. Kevin Greutert. Screenplay by Patrick Melton and Marcus Dunstan. Prod. Gregg Hoffman, Oren Koules, Mark Burg, James Wan, and Leigh Whannell. Perf. Tobin Bell, Costas Mandylor, Mark Rolston. Lions Gate, 2010. DVD.

33 *SAW II.* Dir. Darren L. Bousman. Screenplay by Leigh Whannell and Darren L. Bousman. Prod. Gregg Hoffman, Oren Koules, Mark Burg, and James Wan. Perf. Donnie Wahlberg, Beverley Mitchell, Franky G. Lionsgate, 2006. DVD.

value of life is."[34] Crawling out of the wreckage of his car wounded, but alive, solidified this belief. Kramer began wondering how his body could survive the trauma of the car crash, but not withstand cancer cells.[35] He came to the realization that, even with all of its pain and struggle, life is a beautiful thing. It is a blessing and needs to be cherished. Because of these new discoveries, he once explained: "It was the moment I decided to end my life that started my work and brought meaning to it."[36]

Kramer also realized that he did not have much time and he needed to spend what was left of his life making sure there was a meaningful conclusion.[37] This is similar to the belief expressed by the character Inez in Jean-Paul Sartre's play *No Exit*: "One always dies too soon—or too late. And yet one's whole life is complete at that moment, with a line drawn neatly under it, ready for summing up. You are—your life, and nothing else."[38] Recognizing this, it is implied

34   *SAW VI*. Dir. Kevin Greutert. Screenplay by Patrick Melton and Marcus Dunstan. Prod. Gregg Hoffman, Oren Koules, Mark Burg, James Wan, and Leigh Whannell. Perf. Tobin Bell, Costas Mandylor, Mark Rolston. Lions Gate, 2010. DVD.

35   *SAW II*. Dir. Darren L. Bousman. Screenplay by Leigh Whannell and Darren L. Bousman. Prod. Gregg Hoffman, Oren Koules, Mark Burg, and James Wan. Perf. Donnie Wahlberg, Beverley Mitchell, Franky G. Lionsgate, 2006. DVD.

36   *SAW II*. Dir. Darren L. Bousman. Screenplay by Leigh Whannell and Darren L. Bousman. Prod. Gregg Hoffman, Oren Koules, Mark Burg, and James Wan. Perf. Donnie Wahlberg, Beverley Mitchell, Franky G. Lionsgate, 2006. DVD.

37   *SAW II*. Dir. Darren L. Bousman. Screenplay by Leigh Whannell and Darren L. Bousman. Prod. Gregg Hoffman, Oren Koules, Mark Burg, and James Wan. Perf. Donnie Wahlberg, Beverley Mitchell, Franky G. Lionsgate, 2006. DVD.

38   Solomon, Robert C. *Introducing Philosophy*. Ninth ed. New York: Oxford UP, 2008. qtd. in Solomon 311. Print.

at the end of *SAW II*, by the words of one of Kramer's accomplices, that Kramer wanted to have lived a life that was worthy of remembrance. That was his cure for cancer.[39]

With this new goal, Kramer felt in control and that his life had a purpose again. He began devising ways he could put people in traps where they would be faced with imminent death and would have to learn to help themselves. Unfortunately, Kramer utilized cruel methods in his attempts to enlighten people, drawing on his engineering skills to design and build complicated traps that had to be precisely configured to achieve their objectives. Kramer's engineering brilliance was not affected by his frontal lobe tumor, but his moral reasoning was tragically and severely impaired.[40]

In the end, Kramer died to prove his point. The opportunity to murder Kramer became the final test for a man who was being taught not to take revenge. At the end of *SAW III* and *SAW IV*, which happened concurrently, the test subject failed his test and killed Kramer, an action that condemned the subject and his wife to death.[41]

---

39   *SAW II*. Dir. Darren L. Bousman. Screenplay by Leigh Whannell and Darren L. Bousman. Prod. Gregg Hoffman, Oren Koules, Mark Burg, and James Wan. Perf. Donnie Wahlberg, Beverley Mitchell, Franky G. Lionsgate, 2006. DVD.

40   According to the American Brain Tumor Association, the symptoms of a frontal lobe tumor include "impaired judgment and personality or mental changes;" "Brain Tumor Symptoms." *American Brain Tumor Association*. Web. 05 Dec. 2010. <http://www.abta.org/symptoms/13>.

41   Trap Index, #19B4; *SAW III*. Dir. Darren L. Bousman. Screenplay by Leigh Whannell and Darren L. Bousman. Prod. Gregg Hoffman, Oren Koules, Mark Burg, and James Wan. Perf. Tobin Bell, Shawnee Smith, Angus MacFadyn. Lionsgate, 2007. DVD.

The Puppet

The puppet that Kramer utilized in almost all of his traps was a symbol of Kramer's sorrow and anger. Kramer originally made the puppet for his son, but after the miscarriage he used the puppet to conceal his identity from test victims and law enforcement officials.[42] Kramer continually had the puppet "speak for him" in the instructional tapes he left for his test subjects. The puppet was also used in a variety of other ways, such as riding in on a tricycle to deliver a closing message at the end of a trap or "speaking" as it hung from a noose.[43] In the first case, the puppet represented the child for whom it was created, and in the second case, it represented the death of this child. Both representations are aspects of Kramer's guilt and grief that are continually depicted throughout the series. Though Kramer remained calm and emotionally detached while his games were being played, the puppet was a symbol of the over-whelming sadness he felt.

---

42 *SAW IV*. Dir. Darren L. Bousman. Screenplay by Patrick Melton and Marcus Dunstan. Prod. Gregg Hoffman, Oren Koules, Mark Burg, James Wan, and Leigh Whannell. Perf. Tobin Bell, Scott Patterson, Luis Ferreiera. Lionsgate, 2008. DVD.

43 Trap Index, #7 & #24A2; *SAW*. Dir. James Wan. Screenplay by Leigh Whannell. Prod. Gregg Hoffman, Oren Koules, and Mark Burg. Perf. Leigh Whannell, Carey Elwes, Danny Glover. Lionsgate, 2005. DVD.; *SAW VI*. Dir. Kevin Greutert. Screenplay by Patrick Melton and Marcus Dunstan. Prod. Gregg Hoffman, Oren Koules, Mark Burg, James Wan, and Leigh Whannell. Perf. Tobin Bell, Costas Mandylor, Mark Rolston. Lions Gate, 2010. DVD.

Worst Offender

One of Kramer's traps was literally intended to help viewers feel what Kramer felt. The test subject was the worst offender of any of Kramer's subjects. He was a serial rapist who lived a life of depravity, managing a sleazy hotel. He raped many women, physically abused them in other ways, and took videos and pictures of these violent acts. He was acquitted of rape three times and never paid for his crimes.[44]

Kramer set this trap intentionally to strike a chord, knowing that many people would agree that this subject deserved to be tested in a brutal way. However, in Kramer's view, his other test subjects were just as guilty as the serial rapist, though their sins were different. Through this one stark example, Kramer was demonstrating that, in his view, his traps were appropriate not just for serial rapists, but for everyone who did not cherish their lives or the lives of others, whether they were drug addicts, adulterers, or unsympathetic doctors.

Important Characters

In order to gain further understanding of Kramer, it is essential to examine how he viewed the most important people in his life: his ex-wife and his three accomplices.

44　Trap Index, #20A2a; *SAW IV*. Dir. Darren L. Bousman. Screenplay by Patrick Melton and Marcus Dunstan. Prod. Gregg Hoffman, Oren Koules, Mark Burg, James Wan, and Leigh Whannell. Perf. Tobin Bell, Scott Patterson, Luis Ferreiera. Lionsgate, 2008. DVD.

Jill Tuck. Tuck was Kramer's wife and was a healthcare professional. Her work focused on helping drug addicts. When Kramer was not working, he frequently helped Tuck run her health clinic, where they both dealt with many people who were in desperate need of help. Tuck and Kramer had an excellent marriage and were a good team. The motto of Tuck's health clinic— "Cherish Your Life"—was Kramer's core philosophy of life both before and after his transformation.[45]

Tuck and Kramer carefully planned their family and all was going well until tragedy struck. The loss of their unborn son was the beginning of the end of their marriage. Kramer intentionally drove Tuck away by making her believe that he blamed her for the miscarriage. Kramer made it clear, however, from the message he left for Tuck in his will, that he blamed only himself.[46] One can assume that Kramer was pushing Tuck away only to protect her from his traps and accomplices. Later, after Tuck learned what Kramer was doing, she tried to convince him to stop, but he did not listen. Despite Kramer's transformation and the distance he

45 *SAW IV.* Dir. Darren L. Bousman. Screenplay by Patrick Melton and Marcus Dunstan. Prod. Gregg Hoffman, Oren Koules, Mark Burg, James Wan, and Leigh Whannell. Perf. Tobin Bell, Scott Patterson, Luis Ferreiera. Lionsgate, 2008. DVD.

46 *SAW IV.* Dir. Darren L. Bousman. Screenplay by Patrick Melton and Marcus Dunstan. Prod. Gregg Hoffman, Oren Koules, Mark Burg, James Wan, and Leigh Whannell. Perf. Tobin Bell, Scott Patterson, Luis Ferreiera. Lionsgate, 2008. DVD.; *SAW V.* Dir. David Hackl. Screenplay by Patrick Melton and Marcus Dunstan. Prod. Gregg Hoffman, Oren Koules, Mark Burg, James Wan, and Leigh Whannell. Perf. Scott Patterson, Costas Mandylor, Tobin Bell. Lionsgate, 2009. DVD.

created between himself and Tuck, they never stopped loving each other.

After Kramer was killed, his lawyer summoned Tuck to show her a video and give her a locked box which Kramer had left for her in his will. In the video, Kramer told Tuck that she would know what to do with the contents of the box and ended with, "You are my heart and you always will be." Drying her tears, Tuck unlocked the box using a key Kramer had given her while he was still alive.[47] This box contained the tools Tuck would need to put Kramer's renegade first accomplice in a trap. Tuck followed through, strapping the accomplice to an electrified chair and putting the device around his head. Kramer intended this trap to be unwinnable, but the accomplice managed to escape.[48] Tuck fled the building, but with Kramer's accomplice still alive, she spent the rest of her life in fear and on the run. It was not long before the tables were turned. Kramer's accomplice killed Tuck using a similar device to the one she used on him.[49]

---

47 *SAW V*. Dir. David Hackl. Screenplay by Patrick Melton and Marcus Dunstan. Prod. Gregg Hoffman, Oren Koules, Mark Burg, James Wan, and Leigh Whannell. Perf. Scott Patterson, Costas Mandylor, Tobin Bell. Lionsgate, 2009. DVD.

48 *SAW VI*. Dir. Kevin Greutert. Screenplay by Patrick Melton and Marcus Dunstan. Prod. Gregg Hoffman, Oren Koules, Mark Burg, James Wan, and Leigh Whannell. Perf. Tobin Bell, Costas Mandylor, Mark Rolston. Lions Gate, 2010. DVD.

49 Trap Index, #29; *SAW: The Final Chapter*. Dir. Kevin Greutert. Screenplay by Patrick Melton and Marcus Dunstan. Prod. Gregg Hoffman, Oren Koules, Mark Burg, James Wan, and Leigh Whannell. Perf. Tobin Bell, Costas Mandylor, Besty Russell. Lions Gate, 2010.

Detective Mark Hoffman. Hoffman was one of the
first police detectives assigned to the Jigsaw case. He was
particularly interested in the case because of his own
personal trauma. His sister, who was his only relative, had
been brutally murdered by her boyfriend, Seth Baxter.
After learning about the Jigsaw case, Hoffman decided
to kidnap Baxter and put him in a Jigsaw-style trap.
Although Hoffman deliberately designed this trap to
look like one of Kramer's, Hoffman's trap was intended
for execution as opposed to salvation.[50] After killing
Baxter, Hoffman became an alcoholic consumed with
guilt and shame about his sister and Baxter, driving him
into a sleepless depression.[51]

When Kramer learned about Baxter's execution in
what was supposedly a Jigsaw trap, Kramer kidnapped
Hoffman and offered him a deal by putting him in a
trap.[52] "Now you can arrest me, but doing so, your life
ends as you know it. Or you could explore a method of
rehabilitation that permits you to sleep at night," said
Kramer when he and Hoffman first met face to face.
Either Hoffman would learn Kramer's concept of true

50   Trap Index, #3; *SAW V*. Dir. David Hackl. Screenplay by Patrick
     Melton and Marcus Dunstan. Prod. Gregg Hoffman, Oren
     Koules, Mark Burg, James Wan, and Leigh Whannell. Perf. Scott
     Patterson, Costas Mandylor, Tobin Bell. Lionsgate, 2009. DVD.

51   *SAW V*. Dir. David Hackl. Screenplay by Patrick Melton and
     Marcus Dunstan. Prod. Gregg Hoffman, Oren Koules, Mark
     Burg, James Wan, and Leigh Whannell. Perf. Scott Patterson,
     Costas Mandylor, Tobin Bell. Lionsgate, 2009. DVD.

52   Trap Index, #4; *SAW V*. Dir. David Hackl. Screenplay by Patrick
     Melton and Marcus Dunstan. Prod. Gregg Hoffman, Oren
     Koules, Mark Burg, James Wan, and Leigh Whannell. Perf. Scott
     Patterson, Costas Mandylor, Tobin Bell. Lionsgate, 2009. DVD.

justice and become one of Kramer's apprentices, or Kramer would turn in evidence against Hoffman and Hoffman would spend the rest of his life in jail. Hoffman accepted Kramer's offer, and from that point forward, he worked for Kramer.[53]

Hoffman did not, however, set up every trap properly. Sometimes, he manipulated traps so that they were unwinnable, which Kramer hated and believed was immoral. Kramer was smart enough to see that Hoffman never really took Kramer's teachings to heart and he never considered Hoffman to be a worthy disciple. That is why Kramer set in motion a complex plan to assure that Hoffman would be tested after Kramer died.[54]During the autopsy of Kramer's corpse, the morgue staff found a wax-coated tape in his stomach. Kramer had prepared the tape and swallowed it while on his deathbed. The morgue staff called Hoffman about the tape and he came to the morgue

53 *SAW V*. Dir. David Hackl. Screenplay by Patrick Melton and Marcus Dunstan. Prod. Gregg Hoffman, Oren Koules, Mark Burg, James Wan, and Leigh Whannell. Perf. Scott Patterson, Costas Mandylor, Tobin Bell. Lionsgate, 2009. DVD.

54 *SAW IV*. Dir. Darren L. Bousman. Screenplay by Patrick Melton and Marcus Dunstan. Prod. Gregg Hoffman, Oren Koules, Mark Burg, James Wan, and Leigh Whannell. Perf. Tobin Bell, Scott Patterson, Luis Ferreiera. Lionsgate, 2008. DVD.; *SAW V*. Dir. David Hackl. Screenplay by Patrick Melton and Marcus Dunstan. Prod. Gregg Hoffman, Oren Koules, Mark Burg, James Wan, and Leigh Whannell. Perf. Scott Patterson, Costas Mandylor, Tobin Bell. Lionsgate, 2009. DVD. *SAW: The Final Chapter*. Dir. Kevin Greutert. Screenplay by Patrick Melton and Marcus Dunstan. Prod. Gregg Hoffman, Oren Koules, Mark Burg, James Wan, and Leigh Whannell. Perf. Tobin Bell, Costas Mandylor, Besty Russell. Lions Gate, 2010.

to listen to it. On the tape, Kramer said to Hoffman, "You feel you now have control, don't you? You think you will walk away untested. I promise that my work will continue."[55] This was a clear warning to Hoffman, but he did not heed it.

After Kramer died, Hoffman played the hero and pretended to have captured Kramer. He also continued to move forward with Kramer's work. When Hoffman's traps were discovered, Hoffman, as police detective, pretended to remain on the case, feeling that his hero status would prevent him from being caught.[56] However, he made a critical mistake: when carving a jigsaw puzzle piece from the skin of his victims, he used a different type of knife than Kramer had used. The FBI detected this and discovered Hoffman's true identity as the new Jigsaw killer.[57]

Kramer viewed Hoffman as only a means to an end. Hoffman was an enormous help because he was stronger and healthier than Kramer. Unfortunately, Hoffman never learned to cherish anything, nor to understand and accept the philosophy underlying Kramer's work.

---

55 *SAW IV*. Dir. Darren L. Bousman. Screenplay by Patrick Melton and Marcus Dunstan. Prod. Gregg Hoffman, Oren Koules, Mark Burg, James Wan, and Leigh Whannell. Perf. Tobin Bell, Scott Patterson, Luis Ferreiera. Lionsgate, 2008. DVD.

56 *SAW V*. Dir. David Hackl. Screenplay by Patrick Melton and Marcus Dunstan. Prod. Gregg Hoffman, Oren Koules, Mark Burg, James Wan, and Leigh Whannell. Perf. Scott Patterson, Costas Mandylor, Tobin Bell. Lionsgate, 2009. DVD.

57 *SAW VI*. Dir. Kevin Greutert. Screenplay by Patrick Melton and Marcus Dunstan. Prod. Gregg Hoffman, Oren Koules, Mark Burg, James Wan, and Leigh Whannell. Perf. Tobin Bell, Costas Mandylor, Mark Rolston. Lions Gate, 2010. DVD.

Hoffman was merely the means to Kramer's end of having his selected test subjects kidnapped and trapped. Ironically, Kramer imitated Hoffman by designing an unwinnable trap that was intended to kill Hoffman after Kramer had died.

Amanda Young. Young was a drug addict.[58] She and her boyfriend, Cecil Adams, were patients at Tuck's health clinic. It was Young who set in motion the sequence of events that led to Tuck's traumatic miscarriage. Young badgered Adams to break into the clinic to steal drugs, and during the break-in, Adams slammed a door into Tuck causing the miscarriage.[59] After these events, Young was framed by Detective Eric Mathews and then arrested and convicted for a crime she did not commit. In jail, she developed the habit of cutting her wrists.[60]

As an addict and cutter, Young was an ideal test subject for one of Kramer's traps. Young managed to survive, unlocking the device just before time expired.

---

58   *SAW.* Dir. James Wan. Screenplay by Leigh Whannell. Prod. Gregg Hoffman, Oren Koules, and Mark Burg. Perf. Leigh Whannell, Carey Elwes, Danny Glover. Lionsgate, 2005. DVD.

59   *SAW IV.* Dir. Darren L. Bousman. Screenplay by Patrick Melton and Marcus Dunstan. Prod. Gregg Hoffman, Oren Koules, Mark Burg, James Wan, and Leigh Whannell. Perf. Tobin Bell, Scott Patterson, Luis Ferreiera. Lionsgate, 2008. DVD.; *SAW VI.* Dir. Kevin Greutert. Screenplay by Patrick Melton and Marcus Dunstan. Prod. Gregg Hoffman, Oren Koules, Mark Burg, James Wan, and Leigh Whannell. Perf. Tobin Bell, Costas Mandylor, Mark Rolston. Lions Gate, 2010. DVD.

60   *SAW II.* Dir. Darren L. Bousman. Screenplay by Leigh Whannell and Darren L. Bousman. Prod. Gregg Hoffman, Oren Koules, Mark Burg, and James Wan. Perf. Donnie Wahlberg, Beverley Mitchell, Franky G. Lionsgate, 2006. DVD.

She believed that this experience helped her, taught her that she did care about living, and proved to her that her will to survive was strong.[61] As a result, she stopped using drugs and temporarily stopped cutting herself. She became Kramer's accomplice and began helping him set up traps. Unfortunately, she found Kramer's work to be very emotionally taxing and eventually reverted back to cutting herself. When Kramer discovered this, he placed her in another trap. She survived yet again and, in fact, was one of only two survivors out of the eight test subjects in this trap.[62]

A few days after surviving her second trap, Young captured her arresting officer, Mathews, and locked him in an ankle shackle in a bathroom.[63] Mathews managed to escape the shackle by breaking his foot, and he then confronted Young in the hallway outside the bathroom. After a long fight, Young managed to get away. Despite

61 Trap Index, #7; *SAW*. Dir. James Wan. Screenplay by Leigh Whannell. Prod. Gregg Hoffman, Oren Koules, and Mark Burg. Perf. Leigh Whannell, Carey Elwes, Danny Glover. Lionsgate, 2005. DVD.; *SAW VI*. Dir. Kevin Greutert. Screenplay by Patrick Melton and Marcus Dunstan. Prod. Gregg Hoffman, Oren Koules, Mark Burg, James Wan, and Leigh Whannell. Perf. Tobin Bell, Costas Mandylor, Mark Rolston. Lions Gate, 2010. DVD.

62 Trap Index, #11; *SAW II*. Dir. Darren L. Bousman. Screenplay by Leigh Whannell and Darren L. Bousman. Prod. Gregg Hoffman, Oren Koules, Mark Burg, and James Wan. Perf. Donnie Wahlberg, Beverley Mitchell, Franky G. Lionsgate, 2006. DVD.

63 Trap Index, #15; *SAW II*. Dir. Darren L. Bousman. Screenplay by Leigh Whannell and Darren L. Bousman. Prod. Gregg Hoffman, Oren Koules, Mark Burg, and James Wan. Perf. Donnie Wahlberg, Beverley Mitchell, Franky G. Lionsgate, 2006. DVD.

this harrowing experience, she again regained some stability and returned to work on traps with Kramer.[64]

As Kramer became too weak to set up traps himself, he relied more heavily on Young and Hoffman. This increased dependency on his accomplices allowed Hoffman to rig more and more traps to be unwinnable, but it was Young, because of her emotional instability, who was blamed for the unwinnable traps. Hoffman's betrayal of Kramer's moral lessons caused Young to lose faith in Kramer's tests. She began believing that Kramer's subjects did not deserve a chance to live because they would not actually learn anything from their traps. Young's loss of faith was the reason for her third and final trap.[65] The goal of this trap was to teach Young to control her emotions and get back on the right path.[66]

Young might have passed this final test and regained her faith in Kramer's work if Hoffman had not interfered. Hoffman had learned that Young was partly responsible for the death of Kramer's unborn baby. Knowing that Young would never want Kramer

64 *SAW III*. Dir. Darren L. Bousman. Screenplay by Leigh Whannell and Darren L. Bousman. Prod. Gregg Hoffman, Oren Koules, Mark Burg, and James Wan. Perf. Tobin Bell, Shawnee Smith, Angus MacFadyn. Lionsgate, 2007. DVD.

65 Trap Index, #19; *SAW III*. Dir. Darren L. Bousman. Screenplay by Leigh Whannell and Darren L. Bousman. Prod. Gregg Hoffman, Oren Koules, Mark Burg, and James Wan. Perf. Tobin Bell, Shawnee Smith, Angus MacFadyn. Lionsgate, 2007. DVD.

66 *SAW III*. Dir. Darren L. Bousman. Screenplay by Leigh Whannell and Darren L. Bousman. Prod. Gregg Hoffman, Oren Koules, Mark Burg, and James Wan. Perf. Tobin Bell, Shawnee Smith, Angus MacFadyn. Lionsgate, 2007. DVD.

to learn this dark secret, Hoffman blackmailed
Young into killing Dr. Lynn Denlon, knowing that
her husband, Jeff Denlon, would then take revenge
on Young.[67] The plan worked to perfection. Young
succumbed to both the blackmail and her emotions.
She shot Dr. Denlon just as Jeff Denlon was entering
the room, and Jeff Denlon, reacting true to his
character, immediately shot and killed Young.[68]

The relationship between Young and Kramer was
complex. Sometimes, she seemed to view him as a
father figure or mentor. At other times, Young seemed
romantically inclined toward Kramer. When Kramer
was dying and hallucinating about Tuck, he said "I love
you" to the hallucination, but Young became jealous
and angry because she thought Kramer was talking to
the surgeon, Dr. Denlon, who was caring for him at the
time.[69] *SAW III* director, Darren Lynn Bousman, captured
the essence of this complexity well when he said, "People

---

67 *SAW III*. Dir. Darren L. Bousman. Screenplay by Leigh Whannell
and Darren L. Bousman. Prod. Gregg Hoffman, Oren Koules,
Mark Burg, and James Wan. Perf. Tobin Bell, Shawnee Smith,
Angus MacFadyn. Lionsgate, 2007. DVD.; *SAW IV*. Dir. Darren L.
Bousman. Screenplay by Patrick Melton and Marcus Dunstan.
Prod. Gregg Hoffman, Oren Koules, Mark Burg, James Wan, and
Leigh Whannell. Perf. Tobin Bell, Scott Patterson, Luis Ferreiera.
Lionsgate, 2008. DVD.

68 *SAW III*. Dir. Darren L. Bousman. Screenplay by Leigh Whannell
and Darren L. Bousman. Prod. Gregg Hoffman, Oren Koules,
Mark Burg, and James Wan. Perf. Tobin Bell, Shawnee Smith,
Angus MacFadyn. Lionsgate, 2007. DVD.

69 *SAW III*. Dir. Darren L. Bousman. Screenplay by Leigh Whannell
and Darren L. Bousman. Prod. Gregg Hoffman, Oren Koules,
Mark Burg, and James Wan. Perf. Tobin Bell, Shawnee Smith,
Angus MacFadyn. Lionsgate, 2007. DVD.

look at this movie and I think they see it on the surface. They look at it and they see the violent traps, they see the gore, and they say 'oh it's a gore film.' But there's an extremely … emotional story going on here between Jigsaw and Amanda, and I really urge people to look beneath the surface of the gore."[70] Either way, Young and Kramer were very close. Kramer said of Young: "She swims in my sea. In the end she will be the closest thing I ever got to a connection—to being understood."[71]

Perhaps the character was named "Young" precisely because Kramer viewed her only as a student who was not mature or stable enough to be a teacher. Despite Young's shortcomings, however, Kramer continued to believe in her and continued to provide the periodic encouragement and instruction he believed she needed

70 *SAW III w. Commentary.* Dir. Darren L. Bousman. Screenplay by Leigh Whannell and Darren L. Bousman. Prod. Gregg Hoffman, Oren Koules, Mark Burg, and James Wan. Perf. Tobin Bell, Shawnee Smith, Angus MacFadyn. Lionsgate, 2007. DVD.

71 *SAW III.* Dir. Darren L. Bousman. Screenplay by Leigh Whannell and Darren L. Bousman. Prod. Gregg Hoffman, Oren Koules, Mark Burg, and James Wan. Perf. Tobin Bell, Shawnee Smith, Angus MacFadyn. Lionsgate, 2007. DVD.

to stay on the right path. This is why Kramer felt the need to put her in a total of three traps.[72]

Dr. Lawrence Gordon. Kramer once described Gordon as "a healer who needs some healing."[73] Gordon was a very successful doctor and Kramer's primary care physician. His crimes were cheating on his wife and failing to appreciate his family. In addition, he was very unsympathetic toward his patients, often coldly delivering a very serious diagnosis, such as when he first told Kramer that he had a frontal lobe tumor.[74]

Kramer planted evidence that caused Gordon to become a suspect, hoping that if Gordon learned of

---

72 Trap Index, #7, #11, & #19; *SAW*. Dir. James Wan. Screenplay by Leigh Whannell. Prod. Gregg Hoffman, Oren Koules, and Mark Burg. Perf. Leigh Whannell, Carey Elwes, Danny Glover. Lionsgate, 2005. DVD.; *SAW II*. Dir. Darren L. Bousman. Screenplay by Leigh Whannell and Darren L. Bousman. Prod. Gregg Hoffman, Oren Koules, Mark Burg, and James Wan. Perf. Donnie Wahlberg, Beverley Mitchell, Franky G. Lionsgate, 2006. DVD.; *SAW III*. Dir. Darren L. Bousman. Screenplay by Leigh Whannell and Darren L. Bousman. Prod. Gregg Hoffman, Oren Koules, Mark Burg, and James Wan. Perf. Tobin Bell, Shawnee Smith, Angus MacFadyn. Lionsgate, 2007. DVD.

73 *SAW V*. Dir. David Hackl. Screenplay by Patrick Melton and Marcus Dunstan. Prod. Gregg Hoffman, Oren Koules, Mark Burg, James Wan, and Leigh Whannell. Perf. Scott Patterson, Costas Mandylor, Tobin Bell. Lionsgate, 2009. DVD.

74 *SAW*. Dir. James Wan. Screenplay by Leigh Whannell. Prod. Gregg Hoffman, Oren Koules, and Mark Burg. Perf. Leigh Whannell, Carey Elwes, Danny Glover. Lionsgate, 2005. DVD.

the Jigsaw traps, he might reconsider his life.[75] Upon Gordon's failure to recognize his faults, Kramer kidnapped him and put him in a trap.[76] Though Gordon failed this test, he managed to survive by sawing off his foot, removing his ankle shackle, and crawling out of the bathroom where he had been chained to a pipe.[77] Gordon then cauterized his leg on a hot pipe in the hallway. It was there that Kramer found him, cleaned him up, and took him in as his third and final accomplice.[78]

The final portion of Kramer's plan for Hoffman relied on Gordon. Kramer wanted to make sure that if Hoffman killed Tuck, Gordon would kill Hoffman. After Tuck was killed, Gordon captured Hoffman and chained him in a trap and locked him in the same bathroom, leaving no means of escape. Hoffman was left to die slowly, with Gordon echoing Kramer's infamous words:

75 *SAW*. Dir. James Wan. Screenplay by Leigh Whannell. Prod. Gregg Hoffman, Oren Koules, and Mark Burg. Perf. Leigh Whannell, Carey Elwes, Danny Glover. Lionsgate, 2005. DVD.; *SAW V*. Dir. David Hackl. Screenplay by Patrick Melton and Marcus Dunstan. Prod. Gregg Hoffman, Oren Koules, Mark Burg, James Wan, and Leigh Whannell. Perf. Scott Patterson, Costas Mandylor, Tobin Bell. Lionsgate, 2009. DVD.

76 Trap Index, #10C; *SAW*. Dir. James Wan. Screenplay by Leigh Whannell. Prod. Gregg Hoffman, Oren Koules, and Mark Burg. Perf. Leigh Whannell, Carey Elwes, Danny Glover. Lionsgate, 2005. DVD.

77 *SAW*. Dir. James Wan. Screenplay by Leigh Whannell. Prod. Gregg Hoffman, Oren Koules, and Mark Burg. Perf. Leigh Whannell, Carey Elwes, Danny Glover. Lionsgate, 2005. DVD.

78 *SAW: The Final Chapter*. Dir. Kevin Greutert. Screenplay by Patrick Melton and Marcus Dunstan. Prod. Gregg Hoffman, Oren Koules, Mark Burg, James Wan, and Leigh Whannell. Perf. Tobin Bell, Costas Mandylor, Besty Russell. Lions Gate, 2010.

"Game over."[79] It was sheer poetic justice: the renegade accomplice who built unwinnable traps ended up dying in just such a trap.

Kramer considered Gordon to be his "greatest asset."[80] Like Young, Gordon was a success story—additional proof that Kramer's methods of enlightening worked. Even though Gordon did not pass his test in the manner Kramer intended, he showed that his will to live was very strong. He did what he had to do to escape, going so far as to cut off his own foot. To Kramer, this was sufficient proof that Gordon had learned to cherish his life. In addition, Kramer recognized Gordon as someone who, unlike Young, was mature enough to teach Kramer's philosophy.[81]

Even though Kramer believed in Gordon and knew he would carry out Kramer's final instructions, the bond between Kramer and Gordon was not as emotional as

---

79   Trap Index, #30; *SAW: The Final Chapter*. Dir. Kevin Greutert. Screenplay by Patrick Melton and Marcus Dunstan. Prod. Gregg Hoffman, Oren Koules, Mark Burg, James Wan, and Leigh Whannell. Perf. Tobin Bell, Costas Mandylor, Besty Russell. Lions Gate, 2010.

80   *SAW: The Final Chapter*. Dir. Kevin Greutert. Screenplay by Patrick Melton and Marcus Dunstan. Prod. Gregg Hoffman, Oren Koules, Mark Burg, James Wan, and Leigh Whannell. Perf. Tobin Bell, Costas Mandylor, Besty Russell. Lions Gate, 2010.

81   *SAW*. Dir. James Wan. Screenplay by Leigh Whannell. Prod. Gregg Hoffman, Oren Koules, and Mark Burg. Perf. Leigh Whannell, Carey Elwes, Danny Glover. Lionsgate, 2005. DVD.; *SAW: The Final Chapter*. Dir. Kevin Greutert. Screenplay by Patrick Melton and Marcus Dunstan. Prod. Gregg Hoffman, Oren Koules, Mark Burg, James Wan, and Leigh Whannell. Perf. Tobin Bell, Costas Mandylor, Besty Russell. Lions Gate, 2010.

the bond between Kramer and Young. Though Kramer valued Gordon as a disciple even more than he valued Young, Gordon remained a busy doctor who could not become a full-time apprentice. As a result, Gordon was never as involved in Kramer's work as were Young and Hoffman. Gordon's role was limited to handling the surgical procedures needed for certain traps. However, despite the lesser degree of physical and emotional involvement, Gordon was the only one of Kramer's disciples who became a true teacher and who survived.[82]

---

82   *SAW: The Final Chapter.* Dir. Kevin Greutert. Screenplay by Patrick Melton and Marcus Dunstan. Prod. Gregg Hoffman, Oren Koules, Mark Burg, James Wan, and Leigh Whannell. Perf. Tobin Bell, Costas Mandylor, Besty Russell. Lions Gate, 2010.

Chapter 3:

SEE WHAT HE SEES

To understand the lessons of the *SAW* movies, one must examine Kramer's philosophical framework in order to see the world from Kramer's perspective. Specifically, it is important to understand how Kramer viewed himself, others, morality, karma, and human responsibility.

Himself, Relative to Others

After his transformation, Kramer looked back and saw himself as having been like one of the cave dwellers in Plato's Allegory of the Cave—incapable of moving and only able to see what was ahead.[83] Personal tragedies pulled "him thence by force up the rough and steep path and did not let him go before he was dragged into the sunlight."[84] At first the sunlight blinded Kramer, making him incapable of seeing the truth. It was in this state of blindness that he attempted suicide.[85]

---

83   Arthur, John, and William H. Shaw. *Social and Political Philosophy.* Englewood Cliffs, NJ: Prentice Hall, 1992. Page 455. Print.

84   Arthur, John, and William H. Shaw. *Social and Political Philosophy.* Englewood Cliffs, NJ: Prentice Hall, 1992. Page 456. Print.

85   *SAW II.* Dir. Darren L. Bousman. Screenplay by Leigh Whannell and Darren L. Bousman. Prod. Gregg Hoffman, Oren Koules, Mark Burg, and James Wan. Perf. Donnie Wahlberg, Beverley Mitchell, Franky G. Lionsgate, 2006. DVD.

Once able to see again, Kramer realized that the things outside the cave were cause for what he saw inside the cave.[86] In other words, Kramer realized the most important things in life—cherishing life, the ability to shape one's life, and the will to survive—were what motivated his actions before his transformation. These were the ideas that gave his and Tuck's work meaning.

Kramer returned to the cave and spent the rest of his life attempting to teach the cave dwellers, his test subjects, right from wrong by bestowing his knowledge upon them. He wanted to help his subjects see the light by restoring their will to survive and their value of life. He was, however, ridiculed, denounced and hunted for his actions, because people did not understand his work and his methodology was cruel and ineffective. The people inside the cave even threatened to kill him on occasion, such as his first test subject, Cecil Adams. [87]

When Dr. Gordon and his fellow test subject, Adam Faulkner, woke up chained in a bathroom, it would have been simpler if Kramer had let them awaken with the lights on, but it would not have been symbolic of the process they were supposed to go through. Instead, Kramer had them wake up in the darkness, forcing Gordon to search for the light switch. Kramer was

---

86 Arthur, John, and William H. Shaw. *Social and Political Philosophy*. Englewood Cliffs, NJ: Prentice Hall, 1992. Page 456. Print.

87 Trap Index, #1 and #2; *SAW IV*. Dir. Darren L. Bousman. Screenplay by Patrick Melton and Marcus Dunstan. Prod. Gregg Hoffman, Oren Koules, Mark Burg, James Wan, and Leigh Whannell. Perf. Tobin Bell, Scott Patterson, Luis Ferreiera. Lionsgate, 2008. DVD.; Arthur, John, and William H. Shaw. *Social and Political Philosophy*. Englewood Cliffs, NJ: Prentice Hall, 1992. Page 457. Print.

trying to convince them to leave the cave. Gordon was successful in leaving, while Faulkner was left alone in the dark once again.[88]

People

Both before and after his transformation, Kramer believed in cherishing life, but saw a world full of ungrateful people who did not appreciate their lives or each other. This view was clearly expressed in Kramer's response to a police officer who called him "sick." Kramer replied, "Yes, I'm sick, officer, sick from the disease eating away at me from the inside, sick of people who don't appreciate their blessings, sick of people who scoff at the suffering of others … sick of it all."[89] That is why many of Kramer's subjects were apathetic and uncaring people who had little respect and concern for their own lives and the lives of others.

Faulkner was a perfect example of someone who did not care about himself or other people. He showed a lack of care for the quality of his life when he referred to his apartment as a "shit hole" and seemed rather apathetic about it. When he asked for a cigarette, Dr. Gordon replied, "You really want to stick something you found in this room in your mouth?" Instead of

---

88 Trap Index, #10B, #10C; *SAW*. Dir. James Wan. Screenplay by Leigh Whannell. Prod. Gregg Hoffman, Oren Koules, and Mark Burg. Perf. Leigh Whannell, Carey Elwes, Danny Glover. Lionsgate, 2005. DVD.

89 *SAW*. Dir. James Wan. Screenplay by Leigh Whannell. Prod. Gregg Hoffman, Oren Koules, and Mark Burg. Perf. Leigh Whannell, Carey Elwes, Danny Glover. Lionsgate, 2005. DVD.

reconsidering, Faulkner replied, "Yes, I'm willing to risk it. Give me that sweet cancer."[90] This was particularly offensive to Kramer since he actually knew what it was like to have cancer.

Faulkner cared as little about other people as he did for himself. He made money by stalking others and taking their pictures. He was willing to invade the privacy of anyone his clients wanted him to follow. He would have stalked anyone for money, even people who were not doing anything suspicious and did not deserve to be followed.[91] His apathetic attitude displayed an unacceptable lack of respect and appreciation for other people.

The Pig Mask. The pig mask that Kramer and his disciples wore when they kidnapped a test subject, symbolized the way Kramer saw people of the world. To him, many humans were no better than pigs. They needed to prove themselves by showing the ability to care and the will to survive in order to rise above this status.

The pig mask also symbolized what Kramer thought of himself and his disciples at the time of the kidnapping. Kramer and his disciples only wore the masks when they were kidnapping people, but kidnapping someone to teach them not to kidnap is

---

90   Trap Index, #10B; *SAW.* Dir. James Wan. Screenplay by Leigh Whannell. Prod. Gregg Hoffman, Oren Koules, and Mark Burg. Perf. Leigh Whannell, Carey Elwes, Danny Glover. Lionsgate, 2005. DVD.

91   *SAW.* Dir. James Wan. Screenplay by Leigh Whannell. Prod. Gregg Hoffman, Oren Koules, and Mark Burg. Perf. Leigh Whannell, Carey Elwes, Danny Glover. Lionsgate, 2005. DVD.

paradoxical. So the pig mask also represented Kramer's own moral status while he was kidnapping others.

Morality

Articulating a holistic view of Kramer's morality requires some level of extrapolation to fill in gaps in the ethical principles conveyed by the *SAW* movies. What emerges is that Kramer's moral philosophy is a novel blend of absolute and relative theories.

Moral Relativism is a theory of morality that rejects any general consensus or absolute standard of right and wrong. It holds that ethical standards change according to culture, individual, or time, and that there are no higher standards or beliefs.[92] "There is no criterion, standard, or mark by which to judge except ourselves," and therefore, one cannot determine an action of another person to be wrong because there is no higher good by which to make such a judgment.[93] As Protagoras said, "Man is the measure of all things," and the best ideas are those that can be best defended, whether or not they are actually good ideas.[94] This leads to the conclusion that there is no good or evil because

---

92   Solomon, Robert C. *Introducing Philosophy*. Ninth ed. New York: Oxford UP, 2008. Page 266. Print.; Melchert, Norman. *The Great Conversation*. Fifth ed. 2 Vols. New York: Oxford UP, 2007. Page 44. Print.

93   Melchert, Norman. *The Great Conversation*. Fifth ed. 2 Vols. New York: Oxford UP, 2007. Page 44. Print.

94   Frost, S. E. *Basic Teachings of the Great Philosophers: a Survey of Their Basic Ideas*. New York: Anchor, 1989. Page 83. Print.; Melchert, Norman. *The Great Conversation*. Fifth ed. 2 Vols. New York: Oxford UP, 2007. Page 45. Print.

everything is determined only in relation to each person's or group's point of view, leaving one with a very messy and confusing view of morality.[95]

The ancient Sophists, including Euthydemus, Thrasymachus, and Callicles, similarly taught that morals were merely "convention," a view that many later philosophers would adopt and expand.[96] Gilbert Harman, for instance, is a contemporary philosopher who believes that morals make sense only "with reference to one or another."[97] In other words, moral principles make sense only when a group of people accepts them to be right.

Kramer clearly believed in right and wrong, so he was not a moral relativist. He criticized the ethics of his test subjects based on what he believed were standards of morality that applied to all. This can be seen many times throughout the SAW movies. For example, Kramer told his very first test subject, Cecil Adams: "Today, we're bringing the ugliness inside you out into the open. Now in order for you to stay alive, we have to match your face with the ugliness of your soul."[98] This shows that Kramer was making a judgment on Adams, determining whether his soul was beautiful or ugly. If Kramer were a relativist,

---

95 Frost, S. E. *Basic Teachings of the Great Philosophers: a Survey of Their Basic Ideas.* New York: Anchor, 1989. Page 83. Print.

96 Frost, S. E. *Basic Teachings of the Great Philosophers: a Survey of Their Basic Ideas.* New York: Anchor, 1989. Page 83. Print.

97 Solomon, Robert C. *Introducing Philosophy.* Ninth ed. New York: Oxford UP, 2008. Page 462. Print.

98 Trap Index, #1; *SAW IV.* Dir. Darren L. Bousman. Screenplay by Patrick Melton and Marcus Dunstan. Prod. Gregg Hoffman, Oren Koules, Mark Burg, James Wan, and Leigh Whannell. Perf. Tobin Bell, Scott Patterson, Luis Ferreiera. Lionsgate, 2008. DVD.

such judgments could not be made. Kramer frequently attacked the lack of morality of his test subjects. He would, therefore, disagree with philosophers such as the ancient Sophists and Gilbert Harman.

After the Sophists, Socrates introduced the concept of higher standards. He took morality away from the individual and claimed it laid in knowledge.[99] Kramer definitely believed in a higher standard; otherwise, his choice of test subjects would have had no consistency. Though Kramer never articulated what he believed were the higher standards of morality, his actions strongly suggested that knowledge is the most likely candidate. This is seen in the way Kramer often incorporated scientific and historical information into his philosophical lessons.[100] This is also shown in the way Kramer felt the need to teach morality to his test subjects.

However, a few scenes imply that Kramer might have had some type of belief in God. The creators of *SAW III* purposefully had religious imagery in the background while Kramer was on his deathbed, in order to suggest he held some sort of religious beliefs, without necessarily

---

99 Frost, S. E. *Basic Teachings of the Great Philosophers: a Survey of Their Basic Ideas.* New York: Anchor, 1989. Page 84. Print.

100 *SAW II.* Dir. Darren L. Bousman. Screenplay by Leigh Whannell and Darren L. Bousman. Prod. Gregg Hoffman, Oren Koules, Mark Burg, and James Wan. Perf. Donnie Wahlberg, Beverley Mitchell, Franky G. Lionsgate, 2006. DVD.; *SAW: The Final Chapter*) *SAW: The Final Chapter.* Dir. Kevin Greutert. Screenplay by Patrick Melton and Marcus Dunstan. Prod. Gregg Hoffman, Oren Koules, Mark Burg, James Wan, and Leigh Whannell. Perf. Tobin Bell, Costas Mandylor, Besty Russell. Lions Gate, 2010.

expressing any one in particular.[101] Therefore, some concept of God may have been Kramer's higher standard or may have, at least, influenced his idea of a higher standard.

Though obviously not a relativist, it is clear that Kramer did not believe that moral rules are absolute in every situation. His rules applied in most situations. The idea of murder is the perfect concept to illustrate this point.

Kramer did not believe that he was a murderer, nor did he condone murder. During a test, Kramer told his surgeon, "I despise murderers."[102] Kramer believed that he was merely testing his subjects. If they died, it was their own choice.[103] Even before Dr. Gordon became an accomplice, he recognized this when he said, "The newspapers started calling him 'The Jigsaw Killer.' Actually, technically speaking, he's not really a murderer. He never killed anyone. He finds ways for his victims to kill themselves."[104]

---

101 *SAW III*. Dir. Darren L. Bousman. Screenplay by Leigh Whannell and Darren L. Bousman. Prod. Gregg Hoffman, Oren Koules, Mark Burg, and James Wan. Perf. Tobin Bell, Shawnee Smith, Angus MacFadyn. Lionsgate, 2007. DVD.

102 Trap Index, #19A; *SAW III*. Dir. Darren L. Bousman. Screenplay by Leigh Whannell and Darren L. Bousman. Prod. Gregg Hoffman, Oren Koules, Mark Burg, and James Wan. Perf. Tobin Bell, Shawnee Smith, Angus MacFadyn. Lionsgate, 2007. DVD.

103 *SAW III*. Dir. Darren L. Bousman. Screenplay by Leigh Whannell and Darren L. Bousman. Prod. Gregg Hoffman, Oren Koules, Mark Burg, and James Wan. Perf. Tobin Bell, Shawnee Smith, Angus MacFadyn. Lionsgate, 2007. DVD.

104 *SAW*. Dir. James Wan. Screenplay by Leigh Whannell. Prod. Gregg Hoffman, Oren Koules, and Mark Burg. Perf. Leigh Whannell, Carey Elwes, Danny Glover. Lionsgate, 2005. DVD.

This is why the rigging of tests by Detective Hoffman was repulsive to Kramer. From Kramer's point of view, Hoffman had murdered, while Kramer had not. In fact, Kramer originally targeted Hoffman because of the execution trap Hoffman had set up for the man who killed Hoffman's sister. Hoffman made the trap look like one of Kramer's traps, except it was not a fair trap. It was designed for the man's execution, not his salvation.[105] This was the antithesis of what Kramer was trying to achieve; he never would have designed an unwinnable trap (except for Hoffman himself). When Kramer and Hoffman first met, Kramer made this clear by saying, "But unlike you, I've never killed anyone. I give people a chance." Kramer described his method as "a better, more efficient way."[106]

In the end, however, Kramer instructed Dr. Gordon to condemn Detective Hoffman to death.[107] In this case, it was moral to murder Hoffman because it would prevent him from murdering others. Murdering Hoffman served the greater good, a concept that Kramer's traps frequently encompassed, and it will be discussed in the next chapter.

---

105 Trap Index, #3; *SAW V*. Dir. David Hackl. Screenplay by Patrick Melton and Marcus Dunstan. Prod. Gregg Hoffman, Oren Koules, Mark Burg, James Wan, and Leigh Whannell. Perf. Scott Patterson, Costas Mandylor, Tobin Bell. Lionsgate, 2009. DVD.

106 Trap Index, #4; *SAW V*. Dir. David Hackl. Screenplay by Patrick Melton and Marcus Dunstan. Prod. Gregg Hoffman, Oren Koules, Mark Burg, James Wan, and Leigh Whannell. Perf. Scott Patterson, Costas Mandylor, Tobin Bell. Lionsgate, 2009. DVD.

107 *SAW: The Final Chapter*. Dir. Kevin Greutert. Screenplay by Patrick Melton and Marcus Dunstan. Prod. Gregg Hoffman, Oren Koules, Mark Burg, James Wan, and Leigh Whannell. Perf. Tobin Bell, Costas Mandylor, Besty Russell. Lions Gate, 2010.

In summary, Kramer saw a world in which there are absolute moral rules based on an unspecified higher standard, most likely knowledge. However, these rules could be broken under circumstances when it would benefit the greater good.

Karma

Kramer's views on Karma are similar to Ludwig Wittgenstein's. Wittgenstein believed that good and evil come from one's will and not from the outside world. So "everything just happens as it does happen" and there is no such thing as cosmic rewards or punishments.[108]

Kramer also believed in the randomness of the universe. His views can be best summed up by what he explained to his first test subject before his test: "You see, things aren't sequential. Good doesn't lead to good; nor bad to bad. People steal; don't get caught, live the good life. Others lie and cheat and get elected. Some people stop to help a stranded motorist and get taken out by a speeding semi. There's no accounting for it. How you play the cards you're dealt, that's all that matters."[109] Kramer did not believe in karma because he recognized that good things happen to bad people and bad things happen to good people. He also did not believe that there are explanations for why this happens.

---

108 Melchert, Norman. *The Great Conversation*. Fifth ed. 2 Vols. New York: Oxford UP, 2007. Page 610. Print.
109 *SAW IV*. Dir. Darren L. Bousman. Screenplay by Patrick Melton and Marcus Dunstan. Prod. Gregg Hoffman, Oren Koules, Mark Burg, James Wan, and Leigh Whannell. Perf. Tobin Bell, Scott Patterson, Luis Ferreiera. Lionsgate, 2008. DVD.

If there is no karma, if good is not visited upon those who are good and evil upon those who are evil, then how will good people be rewarded and bad people punished? Kramer's answer was to take these critical tasks upon himself. To Kramer, his subjects had eluded the law or otherwise avoided the consequences of their misdeeds. If nobody or nothing else would punish them, then Kramer would do it himself. Kramer did, however, give subjects the chance to escape by learning the error of their ways and "passing" their tests.

One may then question the point of acting morally in Kramer's world. Wittgenstein provides a possible answer. Wittgenstein believed that some type of happiness came from acting morally, but that this happiness is hard to define because it is not tangible.[110] Kramer clearly believed in the importance of acting morally even though he did not believe in karma. Thus, it is reasonable to conclude that Kramer viewed moral behavior as having some sort of intrinsic value. Otherwise, there would be no reason to act morally. This is an idea that Kramer also shared with the ancient Stoics. To Kramer and the Stoics, doing the right thing is an end in itself.[111]

Responsibility

In ancient times, it was common to believe that people are not free and therefore not responsible for their

---

110 Melchert, Norman. *The Great Conversation*. Fifth ed. 2 Vols. New York: Oxford UP, 2007. Page 611. Print.

111 Russell, Bertrand. "Aristotle's Ethics," "Stoicism," *A History of Western Philosophy*. Fordge Village, Mass: Murray Printing. Page 255. Print.

actions. These ideas evolved into fatalism, the belief that it does not matter what one does, because all actions are predetermined. Everyone meets their fate and it is beyond their control.[112] This theory takes responsibility out of individual hands and puts it into the hands of the universe.[113] If this were so, there would be no need to try to teach, save or punish, because "man is a marionette whose every action is controlled and determined by the pull of strings in the hands of powers far above and beyond him."[114]

Later in history, the concept of predestination was introduced. In this view, God already knows or has already caused every human action.[115] Predestination takes the responsibility out of the hands of the individual and puts it into the hands of God.[116] Therefore, the bad things people do are not their fault, but God's fault. If this were so, there would be no need to try to teach, save, or punish anyone other than God.

A similar theory of human responsibility is the Yoruba philosophy, which holds that at the beginning of each person's life, they choose their "ori" or inner head. Then they arrive on earth with their ori, and it

---

112 Frost, S. E. *Basic Teachings of the Great Philosophers: a Survey of Their Basic Ideas.* New York: Anchor, 1989. Page 128. Print.

113 Solomon, Robert C. *Introducing Philosophy.* Ninth ed. New York: Oxford UP, 2008. Page 389. Print.

114 Frost, S. E. *Basic Teachings of the Great Philosophers: a Survey of Their Basic Ideas.* New York: Anchor, 1989. Page 128. Print.

115 Solomon, Robert C. *Introducing Philosophy.* Ninth ed. New York: Oxford UP, 2008. Page 393. Print.

116 Solomon, Robert C. *Introducing Philosophy.* Ninth ed. New York: Oxford UP, 2008. Page 389. Print.

determines the course of their life.[117] Some heads are badly made, but no one knows which ones they are. People choose their heads blindly.[118] Even though this theory introduces one choice for humans, it does not make humans responsible for their actions because they cannot know whether the ori they choose is good or bad.

Kramer would not agree with fatalism, predestination, or the Yoruba philosophy. If he did, then his efforts to teach, save, or punish others would have been pointless. Kramer placed responsibility squarely on the individual and believed that people are capable of change. Kramer's games were not directed at God or some cosmic force. They were directed at the individual in an attempt to convince his test subjects to change their attitudes and take responsibility for their own lives. Kramer believed that everyone deserved a chance to prove they can change.

Socrates was one of the first philosophers to place some responsibility on humans and to advocate stronger ideas about human freedom.[119] Although Socrates believed that people were on a predetermined path, he also believed that one "could, through knowledge, have some influence upon his destiny."[120] This resonates with Kramer's philosophy in the sense that his traps were intended to bestow knowledge upon his test subjects

117 Solomon, Robert C. *Introducing Philosophy*. Ninth ed. New York: Oxford UP, 2008. Page 397. Print.

118 Solomon, Robert C. *Introducing Philosophy*. Ninth ed. New York: Oxford UP, 2008. Page 398. Print.

119 Frost, S. E. *Basic Teachings of the Great Philosophers: a Survey of Their Basic Ideas*. New York: Anchor, 1989. Page 130. Print.

120 Frost, S. E. *Basic Teachings of the Great Philosophers: a Survey of Their Basic Ideas*. New York: Anchor, 1989. Page 131. Print.

that would empower them to change their destinies. Kramer's view of freedom, however, was more expansive than Socrates' view, in that Kramer did not believe that people were on a predetermined path. He believed his test subjects made the choices that got them in trouble in the first place and this is why the traps were so harsh. If Kramer had believed in predetermined paths that could merely be influenced by knowledge, perhaps his tests would not have been as brutal.

Plato advocated a more complete theory of free will. He believed that in order to live the good life, one must be free because one who is free can build a satisfying life.[121] Similarly, Epicurus concluded that people have free will. Being an atomist, he looked to atoms first in order to develop a free will theory. Epicurus recognized that atoms are free and have the ability to be spontaneous.[122] Therefore, so do humans. Kramer would have agreed with both of these ideas. Kramer's work was based on the view that people are free and have the power to shape their lives.

Determinism is a more refined version of fatalism. Determinism is based on the "principle of universal causation," describing a world that is ruled by laws of nature that determine everything down to what one thinks.[123] Philosophers such as Thomas Hobbes

121 Frost, S. E. *Basic Teachings of the Great Philosophers: a Survey of Their Basic Ideas.* New York: Anchor, 1989. Page 131. Print.

122 Frost, S. E. *Basic Teachings of the Great Philosophers: a Survey of Their Basic Ideas.* New York: Anchor, 1989. Pages 132-133. Print.;

123 Solomon, Robert C. *Introducing Philosophy.* Ninth ed. New York: Oxford UP, 2008. Page 402. Print.; Melchert, Norman. *The Great Conversation.* Fifth ed. 2 Vols. New York: Oxford UP, 2007. Page 413. Print.

argued that the world and everything in it could be explained through mechanical cause and effect, action and reaction sequences.[124] David Hume believed one could see this concept at work by simply observing the world around them. There are actions and reactions happening all the time and usually with uniformity.[125] If determinism were true, the laws of nature would determine everything one thinks, feels, says and does.

Kramer would generally disagree with determinism, especially with respect to the universe and the soul, but he seemed to adopt a deterministic position in one specific way. While he and Detective Hoffman were setting up a trap, Kramer explained, "If you're good at anticipating the human mind, it leaves nothing to chance."[126] Since Kramer did not distinguish between the mind and the brain, one may assume he was referring to the material brain. This implicitly expresses a view in which there are laws governing the human brain. If not, there would be no way to anticipate what the human brain does. The problem arises when one tries to reconcile Kramer's view of the deterministic quality of the human brain with his belief in free will that was inherent in the way he designed his traps. René Descartes had a solution that best fits with Kramer's view of the world.

---

124 Frost, S. E. *Basic Teachings of the Great Philosophers: a Survey of Their Basic Ideas.* New York: Anchor, 1989. Page 140. Print.

125 Frost, S. E. *Basic Teachings of the Great Philosophers: a Survey of Their Basic Ideas.* New York: Anchor, 1989. Page 143. Print.

126 Trap Index, #11; *SAW V.* Dir. David Hackl. Screenplay by Patrick Melton and Marcus Dunstan. Prod. Gregg Hoffman, Oren Koules, Mark Burg, James Wan, and Leigh Whannell. Perf. Scott Patterson, Costas Mandylor, Tobin Bell. Lionsgate, 2009. DVD.

Descartes accepted determinism in terms of the universe and the human body. He differentiated, however, between the body and the mind or soul.[127] From his point of view, the body may have been determined, but the soul and the will are free.[128] Because the will has absolute freedom, like God's, it can influence the body, but otherwise the body is subject to the deterministic universe.[129]

Since the material brain is a part of the body, Kramer, like Descartes, believed it was subject to determinism. The soul is what Kramer believed could influence the determined body, and it is the soul, not the body, that Kramer judged as either "beautiful" or "ugly" in a moral sense. Unlike Descartes, however, Kramer did not seem to believe that the universe is determined.

John Locke also believed in the human ability to generally do what they want, but to sometimes be unable to stop doing or not doing something.[130] Hume explained something similar by attempting to describe a way in which humans could have aspects of both determinism and free will. He believed if an action is consistent with an individual's nature, it is a free action,

---

127 Frost, S. E. *Basic Teachings of the Great Philosophers: a Survey of Their Basic Ideas.* New York: Anchor, 1989. Page 140. Print.

128 Melchert, Norman. *The Great Conversation.* Fifth ed. 2 Vols. New York: Oxford UP, 2007. Page 413. Print.

129 Melchert, Norman. *The Great Conversation.* Fifth ed. 2 Vols. New York: Oxford UP, 2007. Page 445. Print.; Frost, S. E. *Basic Teachings of the Great Philosophers: a Survey of Their Basic Ideas.* New York: Anchor, 1989. Page 141. Print.

130 Frost, S. E. *Basic Teachings of the Great Philosophers: a Survey of Their Basic Ideas.* New York: Anchor, 1989. Page 143. Print.

but if it is contrary to the individual's nature, it must have been a determined action.[131]

Kramer's philosophy is a unique form of compatibilism, the view of human responsibility that incorporates both elements of determinism and elements of human freedom.[132] In Kramer's philosophy, the human body is determined in the way it responds to the random universe, giving Kramer the ability to predict how people will react on an instinctive or emotional level. The human soul, however, has the ability to influence the body and stop its deterministic nature, giving freedom and responsibility to the individual.

---

131 Frost, S. E. *Basic Teachings of the Great Philosophers: a Survey of Their Basic Ideas.* New York: Anchor, 1989. Page 144. Print.

132 Solomon, Robert C. *Introducing Philosophy.* Ninth ed. New York: Oxford UP, 2008. Page 414. Print.

Chapter 4:

SAVE AS HE SAVES

T he *SAW* series teaches three primary lessons: everyone should cherish their life and the lives of others, determine yet accept their own identities, and grasp the significance of the will to survive. These messages are grounded in Kramer's experiences and view of the world, as well as his philosophical framework.[133] A thorough analysis of these messages, with detailed examples, will provide a foundation to spread Kramer's good messages to others, or to "save as he saves."

Identity[134]

Kramer's views on identity are similar to those of an existentialist, but he is not actually an existentialist. When Sartre generalized existentialist philosophers, he said, "What they have in common is simply that fact that they believe existence comes before essence."[135]

---

133 As expressed in Chapter 2 and 3

134 The message about cherishing life is the single most important lesson of the movies. Because that message is predicated on Kramer's lessons about identity, the subject of identity is addressed first.

135 Flew, Antony. "Essence and Existence: Existentialism." *An Introduction to Western Philosophy: Ideas and Argument from Plato to Sartre.* Indianapolis, New York: Bobbs-Merrill, 1971. Pages 462-463. Print.

Sartre then went on to describe essence as "the formulae and qualities which made its production and its definition possible."[136] Thus, the existentialist thinks that people are blank slates when they come into existence and then they define themselves throughout their lives. This entails that there is no human nature and, therefore, no general laws that guide human action.[137] It is this last point that distinguishes pure existentialism from Kramer's theory of identity. Because of his deterministic view of the human brain, Kramer would not agree that there is neither human nature nor laws that guide human action.

However, even though Kramer disagreed with one main tenet of existentialism, he fully endorsed other core existentialist themes such as "freedom, decision, and responsibility."[138] There are three main existentialist points in Kramer's philosophy. First, he believed that people are able to shape their lives however they want. Second, he believed that the facts of one's life are not enough to determine identity. Third, he believed that it is unhealthy to live in what Sartre called "bad faith."

Defining One's Existence. Existentialism frequently stresses the importance of the individual and the principles that one can determine one's life, make

136 Flew, Antony. "Essence and Existence: Existentialism." *An Introduction to Western Philosophy: Ideas and Argument from Plato to Sartre.* Indianapolis, New York: Bobbs-Merrill, 1971. Page 463. Print.

137 Flew, Antony. "Essence and Existence: Existentialism." *An Introduction to Western Philosophy: Ideas and Argument from Plato to Sartre.* Indianapolis, New York: Bobbs-Merrill, 1971. Page 465. Print.

138 Macquarrie, John. *Existentialism.* Penguin, 1972. Page 4. Print.

oneself happy, and build a life that can be cherished.[139] This philosophy put an "enormous emphasis on the scope and significance of human decision."[140] This is something on which Kramer also focused a great deal.

Kramer believed that people are able to make of themselves what they want. This is similar to the teachings of existentialist philosophers such as Sartre, Martin Heidegger, and Karl Jaspers, who all believed that "man can define his existence."[141] This is important in Kramer's philosophy and provides a reason for why he did what he did. If people can make of themselves what they want, then it was the fault of his test subjects that they behaved in a way that caused Kramer to put them in traps. By extension, Kramer believed his traps had the potential to work because people can change and reshape their lives however they want. Kramer would strongly agree with Sartre's position that "man is nothing else but that which he makes of himself."[142]

Wholeness of Identity. Like the existentialists, Kramer believed that one's identity is not made up of only the facts of one's life.[143] Kramer clearly distinguishes between actions and intentions, and it is obvious that actions

139 Frost, S. E. *Basic Teachings of the Great Philosophers: a Survey of Their Basic Ideas.* New York: Anchor, 1989. Page 265. Print.

140 Flew, Antony. *An Introduction to Western Philosophy: Ideas and Argument from Plato to Sartre.* Indianapolis, New York: Bobbs-Merrill, 1971. Page 462. Print.

141 Frost, S. E. *Basic Teachings of the Great Philosophers: a Survey of Their Basic Ideas.* New York: Anchor, 1989. Page 265. Print.

142 Solomon, Robert C. *Introducing Philosophy.* Ninth ed. New York: Oxford UP, 2008. Page 307. Print.

143 Solomon, Robert C. *Introducing Philosophy.* Ninth ed. New York: Oxford UP, 2008. Page 307. Print.

alone do not, in his view, give a full picture of one's identity. In order to determine identity, one must judge what Sartre called "transcendence," which includes a person's "ambitions, plans, intentions, hopes, and fantasies," as well as the facts about a person's life.[144] Taking into account only one of these things can never be sufficient to determine a person's identity. "He cannot be pieced together from thought, feeling, and will. These are abstractions from the whole."[145]

A good example of this type of existentialist thought can be seen in Kramer's treatment of Detective Mathews. Mathews had been suspended due to use of excessive force.[146] After this suspension, it is implied that Mathews began acting a little more cautiously, but during his trap, Mathews reverted back to his old ways, implying that he never really desired to act morally.[147] His lack of remorse and continued bad intentions were among the many reasons why Kramer put him in a trap. In this case, the fact that Mathews had begun to act ethically was not sufficient enough for Kramer. This trap showed that Mathews' intentions mattered as well. Judging Mathews by the improvement in his behavior would have been an inadequate way to judge his character to Kramer.

---

144 Solomon, Robert C. *Introducing Philosophy*. Ninth ed. New York: Oxford UP, 2008. Page 308. Print.

145 Macquarrie, John. *Existentialism*. Penguin, 1972. Page 135. Print.

146 *Full Disclosure Report: Piecing Together Jigsaw*. Lions Gate, 2005. DVD.

147 *SAW II*. Dir. Darren L. Bousman. Screenplay by Leigh Whannell and Darren L. Bousman. Prod. Gregg Hoffman, Oren Koules, Mark Burg, and James Wan. Perf. Donnie Wahlberg, Beverley Mitchell, Franky G. Lionsgate, 2006. DVD.

Bad Faith. Like Sartre, Kramer also realized the dangers of living in "bad faith." Bad faith can be achieved in two ways: by not accepting one's identity, or by accepting one's identity as something that is unchangeable.[148]

One of the most prominent examples of Kramer attempting to help someone recognize their identity is when he took on Detective Hoffman as an accomplice during Hoffman's first test.[149] In this trap, there was a mirror across from the chair in which Hoffman sat. Kramer wanted Hoffman to look in the mirror and realize what he had become since his sister's death. Kramer's intentions were to not only make Hoffman realize that he had become a killer, but also to get Hoffman to realize his true intentions and desires, thus taking a very existentialist approach.[150]

Kramer's disapproval of people who feel their identity is unchangeable was illustrated in a particular trap. The aim of this trap was for an abused wife to literally detach herself from her abusive husband, saving

---

148 Solomon, Robert C. *Introducing Philosophy*. Ninth ed. New York: Oxford UP, 2008. Page 309. Print.

149 . Trap Index, #4; *SAW V*. Dir. David Hackl. Screenplay by Patrick Melton and Marcus Dunstan. Prod. Gregg Hoffman, Oren Koules, Mark Burg, James Wan, and Leigh Whannell. Perf. Scott Patterson, Costas Mandylor, Tobin Bell. Lionsgate, 2009. DVD.

150 Trap Index, #3; *SAW V*. Dir. David Hackl. Screenplay by Patrick Melton and Marcus Dunstan. Prod. Gregg Hoffman, Oren Koules, Mark Burg, James Wan, and Leigh Whannell. Perf. Scott Patterson, Costas Mandylor, Tobin Bell. Lionsgate, 2009. DVD.

her life, but ending his.[151] This trap is symbolic of how Kramer viewed the wife's life. She was living in bad faith because of her inability to give up her identity as the wife of an abusive husband. This was one of the rare traps that worked; the test subject escaped and we are left to assume her life was better afterwards.

Cherish Your Life

Democritus, a Greek atomist, "taught that the goal of life is happiness," an idea with which many philosophers would agree.[152] The main lesson of Kramer's philosophy was that people should learn to be happy with their lives, accepting both the good and the bad for what they are. People should count their blessings and be thankful for every day they are alive. This may be accomplished by learning to see the intrinsic value of life itself, something that also was important to Aristotle.[153] Kramer's views are consistent with the views of Aristotle and many other philosophers who believed that the highest good was happiness.[154]

---

151 Trap Index, #20A3a; *SAW IV.* Dir. Darren L. Bousman. Screenplay by Patrick Melton and Marcus Dunstan. Prod. Gregg Hoffman, Oren Koules, Mark Burg, James Wan, and Leigh Whannell. Perf. Tobin Bell, Scott Patterson, Luis Ferreiera. Lionsgate, 2008. DVD.

152 Frost, S. E. *Basic Teachings of the Great Philosophers: a Survey of Their Basic Ideas.* New York: Anchor, 1989. Page 82. Print.

153 Frost, S. E. *Basic Teachings of the Great Philosophers: a Survey of Their Basic Ideas.* New York: Anchor, 1989. Page 85. Print.

154 Russell, Bertrand. *A History of Western Philosophy.* Fordge Village, Mass: Murray Printing. Pages 173, 178. Print.

Because of his views on the value of life, Kramer believed very strongly in the importance of cherishing one's body. People who intentionally hurt themselves deserved to be tested because acts of masochism, to Kramer, showed a lack of appreciation for life. Kramer did not distinguish between a masochist trying to draw attention to himself and a masochist truly attempting suicide. He believed that all people need to respect their bodies in order to deserve to live.

This philosophy was reflected particularly well in a specific trap. The instructional recording for the trap was: "Hello, Paul. You are a perfectly healthy, sane, middle class male. Yet last month, you ran a straight razor across your wrist. Did you cut yourself because you truly wanted to die, or did you just want some attention? Tonight you'll show me. The irony is that if you want to die, you just have to stay where you are, but if you want to live, you'll have to cut yourself again. Find the path through the razor wire to the door. But hurry. At three o'clock that door will lock and this room will become your tomb. How much blood will you shed to stay alive, Paul?" That final question became one of the most iconic lines of the *SAW* series.[155]

Kramer's Eight-Fold Path

In Kramer's system of ethics, there are eight ways to reach the highest good of happiness, and the

---

155 Trap Index, #5; *SAW*. Dir. James Wan. Screenplay by Leigh Whannell. Prod. Gregg Hoffman, Oren Koules, and Mark Burg. Perf. Leigh Whannell, Carey Elwes, Danny Glover. Lionsgate, 2005. DVD.

combination of all of them produces the greatest happiness. Kramer's existentialist view of identity is what makes this all possible because it entails that people are always capable of finding a way to do these eight actions and to shape their lives in the best way possible. If people can follow this path, they can cherish every moment, even before they are confronted with life-threatening circumstances.

Act Morally. Acting morally brings about happiness, something Aristotle advocated.[156] Aristotle follows this by saying people cannot befriend themselves unless they are good: "Wicked men, he asserts, often hate themselves."[157] Kramer clearly would have agreed with Aristotle. This is seen in the nature of Kramer's traps. Most of his traps were created in order to teach morality to the test subjects with the hope that if they passed their tests, their lives would be significantly better and they would be happier.

The most concrete example of this type of thinking is seen in Kramer's treatment of Detective Hoffman. Kramer attempted to teach morality to Hoffman with the ultimate goal of making him happier. Kramer mentions that after Hoffman killed Seth Baxter, he did not sleep and spent every night drinking at a bar.[158]

---

156 Russell, Bertrand. *A History of Western Philosophy*. Fordge Village, Mass: Murray Printing. Pages 173. Print.

157 Russell, Bertrand. *A History of Western Philosophy*. Fordge Village, Mass: Murray Printing. qtd. in Russell 180. Print.

158 *SAW V.* Dir. David Hackl. Screenplay by Patrick Melton and Marcus Dunstan. Prod. Gregg Hoffman, Oren Koules, Mark Burg, James Wan, and Leigh Whannell. Perf. Scott Patterson, Costas Mandylor, Tobin Bell. Lionsgate, 2009. DVD.

Kramer considered his own way of doing things to be "a method of rehabilitation that permits you to sleep at night."[159] If Hoffman had adopted Kramer's methods and acted in-tune with what Kramer believed was sound morality, then Hoffman could have finally been at peace with himself.

Have Good Intentions. One needs to have good intentions in order to be happy. To Kramer, acting morally was important, but not sufficient. He was also concerned with intentions. This relates back to Kramer's belief that actions are not sufficient in order to judge one's life. Though the existentialists extended judgment into all area's of one's life, they were not the only philosophers who advocated that intentions matter as much as actions.

Democritus taught that "the good man is not one who does good, but one who wants to do good at all times."[160] Aristotle believed that people who come to self-realization would both act well and want to act well, without being forced to do so.[161] Johann Gottlieb Fichte thought that one must become intelligent so they can do right, and that intelligence would give one the desire to do right.[162]

---

159 *SAW V.* Dir. David Hackl. Screenplay by Patrick Melton and Marcus Dunstan. Prod. Gregg Hoffman, Oren Koules, Mark Burg, James Wan, and Leigh Whannell. Perf. Scott Patterson, Costas Mandylor, Tobin Bell. Lionsgate, 2009. DVD.

160 Frost, S. E. *Basic Teachings of the Great Philosophers: a Survey of Their Basic Ideas.* New York: Anchor, 1989. Page 82. Print.

161 Frost, S. E. *Basic Teachings of the Great Philosophers: a Survey of Their Basic Ideas.* New York: Anchor, 1989. Page 86. Print.

162 Frost, S. E. *Basic Teachings of the Great Philosophers: a Survey of Their Basic Ideas.* New York: Anchor, 1989. Page 96. Print.

Immanuel Kant went to an extreme and claimed that the consequences of an action did not matter; only the intentions of an act should be taken into account when judging its morality: "According to Kant we cannot justify the morality of our actions simply by appealing to the good consequences of our actions for others or ourselves."[163] Since Kramer seemed to focus on the consequences of actions, one cannot say that he would have completely agreed with Kant's position, but he certainly would have agreed that having good intentions is very important.

Again, one may return to the example of Detective Mathews. Mathews could not be judged by the fact that his behavior had improved. Kramer could tell that on the inside, Mathews was acting well behaved only because he had gotten in trouble. In this case, Mathews' intentions provided far more insight into his character than his actions. Mathews showed his true colors by assaulting Kramer at the end of his trap.

Do Not Take The Easy Way Out. Kramer did not believe that life was easy; he believed that it was bad for one to attempt to circumvent life's struggles and obstacles by cheating and taking the easy way out. Drug abuse, masochism, and stealing are but a few activities that Kramer was against because they are ways of escaping life's struggles. In this way, Kramer's traps reflected life as he understood it—painful and difficult, but worth getting through. To Kramer, neither his traps nor life

163 Frost, S. E. *Basic Teachings of the Great Philosophers: a Survey of Their Basic Ideas.* New York: Anchor, 1989. Pages 94-95. Print.; Solomon, Robert C. *Introducing Philosophy.* Ninth ed. New York: Oxford UP, 2008. Page 458. Print.

rewarded people who took the easy way out. Kramer's traps imparted the lesson that the longer and more difficult route is the more fulfilling one.

Sometimes test subjects noticed this, and other times they did not. Dr. Gordon realized it when he said to his fellow test subject, "He doesn't want us to cut through our chains. He wants us to cut through our feet." However, this did not stop Gordon from subsequently attempting to cheat his way out of the trap, an action for which his fellow test subject was punished.[164]

Live A Life of Reason. People can make good decisions and be happy with them by living a life of reason. Plato believed that the highest good—happiness—could be found in a life of reason, where one's desires are governed by logical thinking. This is the path of someone who has "wisdom, courage, and self-control."[165] People who cannot control themselves lose their ability to reason well and thus make poor choices based on instinct. This is why a life of reason was just as important to Plato as it was to Kramer.

This philosophy has a strong presence in almost all of Kramer's traps. Many of Kramer's test subjects seem to be controlled by some outside force. Whether it was drugs, lust, depression, or an obsession—Kramer felt that these problems precluded people from being in control

---

164 Trap Index, #10B & 10C; *SAW*. Dir. James Wan. Screenplay by Leigh Whannell. Prod. Gregg Hoffman, Oren Koules, and Mark Burg. Perf. Leigh Whannell, Carey Elwes, Danny Glover. Lionsgate, 2005. DVD.
165 Frost, S. E. *Basic Teachings of the Great Philosophers: a Survey of Their Basic Ideas.* New York: Anchor, 1989. Pages 85, 84. Print.

of their lives and, therefore, left them unable to live a life of reason.

One of the best examples of Kramer's concept of a life of reason can be found in a very simple test, which was set up in Kramer's lair. When the two detectives, David Tapp and Steven Sing, entered Kramer's lair, Kramer set off a trap that could have killed an innocent man in 20 seconds. Tapp and Sing had to decide whether or not to arrest Kramer or save the innocent man.[166]

This trap was a struggle mostly for Tapp, who had become obsessed with Kramer's case. This trap was meant to teach Tap that saving an innocent life was always more important and that his obsession with arresting Kramer should never outweigh that. If Tapp and Sing had failed to save the man in the trap, their lives would have been made even worse. It would have meant that they were letting an outside force control them, preventing them from making wise decisions and living a life of reason.

Be Self-fulfilling. Kramer believed that people should be able to make themselves happy and not be dependent on outside factors. Democritus is among the philosophers who taught that "things of the world" should not determine one's happiness. The reason why one should not depend on such things is because things of the world are not permanent. If one's happiness

---

166 Trap Index, #8; *SAW*. Dir. James Wan. Screenplay by Leigh Whannell. Prod. Gregg Hoffman, Oren Koules, and Mark Burg. Perf. Leigh Whannell, Carey Elwes, Danny Glover. Lionsgate, 2005. DVD.

depends on them, then one's happiness is just as impermanent.[167]

To understand Kramer's views on self-fulfillment it is helpful to consider his stance on drug abuse. Kramer believed it was possible for addiction to be a part of human nature, but it was something everyone should resist.[168] If one becomes addicted to drugs, then their pleasure or so-called happiness is dependent on the substance and not on themselves. The absence of these drugs then leads to dissatisfaction and withdrawal, showing that one's self-fulfillment has become reliant on an outside substance.

Choose Happiness Over Pleasure. One must pursue happiness over pleasure. Kramer's philosophy reflected that of Aristotle's in how he clearly distinguished between happiness and pleasure.[169] Pleasure may give one the sense that they are happy, but it does not promote happiness in the long run.[170] However, not all pleasure is bad. To both Aristotle and Kramer, happiness lies in self-realization, and pleasure "is a natural result of such realization."[171]

167 Frost, S. E. *Basic Teachings of the Great Philosophers: a Survey of Their Basic Ideas.* New York: Anchor, 1989. Page 86. Print.

168 *SAW VI.* Dir. Kevin Greutert. Screenplay by Patrick Melton and Marcus Dunstan. Prod. Gregg Hoffman, Oren Koules, Mark Burg, James Wan, and Leigh Whannell. Perf. Tobin Bell, Costas Mandylor, Mark Rolston. Lions Gate, 2010. DVD.

169 Russell, Bertrand. *A History of Western Philosophy.* Fordge Village, Mass: Murray Printing. Page 180. Print.

170 Melchert, Norman. *The Great Conversation.* Fifth ed. 2 Vols. New York: Oxford UP, 2007. Page 187. Print.

171 Frost, S. E. *Basic Teachings of the Great Philosophers: a Survey of Their Basic Ideas.* New York: Anchor, 1989. Page 85. Print.

Taking a somewhat different stance, Epicurus promoted pleasure as the cause of happiness, something that seems to contradict what Kramer believed. However, Epicurus further explained that some pleasures are dangerous. They are dangerous in the sense that they do not promote future happiness.[172] In this sense, Epicurus' beliefs are fairly similar to those of Aristotle and Kramer, but he reached his conclusion in a different way.

The difference between happiness and pleasure is reflected in Kramer's choice of subjects. He often targeted people who valued pleasure over happiness, but never targeted anyone who valued the pleasure that comes with happiness. One can assume that Kramer would have believed that pleasure is bad only when it is valued above happiness.

Dr. Gordon is a good example of someone who was trapped for valuing pleasure over happiness.[173] On the night Gordon was kidnapped, he was on his way to continue the affair he was having with his intern, when his wife stopped him and asked, "How can you walk through life pretending that you're happy?"[174] This shows that his happiness was only a charade. Gordon's wife was the one who could ultimately make him happy,

172 Frost, S. E. *Basic Teachings of the Great Philosophers: a Survey of Their Basic Ideas.* New York: Anchor, 1989. Page 86. Print.

173 . Trap Index, #10C; *SAW.* Dir. James Wan. Screenplay by Leigh Whannell. Prod. Gregg Hoffman, Oren Koules, and Mark Burg. Perf. Leigh Whannell, Carey Elwes, Danny Glover. Lionsgate, 2005. DVD.

174 *SAW.* Dir. James Wan. Screenplay by Leigh Whannell. Prod. Gregg Hoffman, Oren Koules, and Mark Burg. Perf. Leigh Whannell, Carey Elwes, Danny Glover. Lionsgate, 2005. DVD.

but he chose to have an affair, showing a preference for pleasure over happiness.

Keep Calm and Remain Stoic. Following certain principles of stoicism will help one be happy. Kramer agreed with some but not all ideas of the original Stoics. The overlaps are seen in the way Kramer attempted to teach people to simply live in harmony with the universe, take a calm and logical approach to each situation, and not let bad events affect them so deeply that they stop taking care of themselves. Both Kramer and the Stoics believed that "man's highest good lay in acting in harmony with the universe."[175]

For example, Kramer attempted to show two police officers that it was better to let his games play out, rather than interfering because they were obsessed with saving everyone and solving the case.[176] When their obsessions led them to intervene, it resulted in more games, more tragedy, and eventually their own deaths. The highest good, to Kramer, would have been for them to simply act in harmony with the bad things that were going on around them, by not letting such events destroy their happiness and quality of life.

---

175 (Frost, S. E. *Basic Teachings of the Great Philosophers: a Survey of Their Basic Ideas.* New York: Anchor, 1989. Page 86. Print.

176 Trap Index, #17 and #20A; *SAW III.* Dir. Darren L. Bousman. Screenplay by Leigh Whannell and Darren L. Bousman. Prod. Gregg Hoffman, Oren Koules, Mark Burg, and James Wan. Perf. Tobin Bell, Shawnee Smith, Angus MacFadyn. Lionsgate, 2007. DVD.; *SAW IV.* Dir. Darren L. Bousman. Screenplay by Patrick Melton and Marcus Dunstan. Prod. Gregg Hoffman, Oren Koules, Mark Burg, James Wan, and Leigh Whannell. Perf. Tobin Bell, Scott Patterson, Luis Ferreiera. Lionsgate, 2008. DVD.

Another example of this philosophy can be seen in Kramer's own actions. Nothing seemed to stir Kramer. He remained calm and tried to teach others to do the same. This is because Kramer acted in harmony with what was going on around him and there are a number of scenes throughout the series that show Kramer "going with the flow" even when bad things were happening. Even when Detective Mathews became hysterical during his test and beat Kramer nearly to death, Kramer still never lost his composure.[177]

The Stoics also taught "everything really good or bad in a man's life depends upon himself."[178] This lesson was the one Kramer was trying to teach Young in her third and final test.[179] "But her emotion is also her weakness," Kramer said, explaining his reason for testing her a third time. This is also why, as Kramer was dying of cancer, he did not want Young to be so upset. To Kramer, his death would be a tragedy to her only if she allowed it to be. He wanted her to learn to control her emotions and accept what happened in her life.

Kramer would not agree with the Stoics' ideas of human freedom. To the Stoics, part of being in harmony with the universe was accepting everything as predetermined. The Stoics believed there was no possible

177 Trap Index, #14; *SAW II*. Dir. Darren L. Bousman. Screenplay by Leigh Whannell and Darren L. Bousman. Prod. Gregg Hoffman, Oren Koules, Mark Burg, and James Wan. Perf. Donnie Wahlberg, Beverley Mitchell, Franky G. Lionsgate, 2006. DVD.

178 Russell, Bertrand. *A History of Western Philosophy*. Fordge Village, Mass: Murray Printing. Page 255. Print.

179 Trap Index, #19; *SAW III*. Dir. Darren L. Bousman. Screenplay by Leigh Whannell and Darren L. Bousman. Prod. Gregg Hoffman, Oren Koules, Mark Burg, and James Wan. Perf. Tobin Bell, Shawnee Smith, Angus MacFadyn. Lionsgate, 2007. DVD.

way of changing the way things played out.[180] To the contrary, Kramer believed that people should act in harmony with the universe, but not because everything is predetermined. He believed that humans do have the ability to cause change, but should not always try. Some of life's struggles must be accepted; refusing to accept them may only cause more struggle.

Cherish the Lives of Others. Cherishing the lives of others is an important part of building a happy life for oneself. It is almost as important as cherishing one's own life. Kramer taught that one should not use other people, but try to see the intrinsic value in relationships. He believed that being sympathetic and caring toward others was extremely important. Kramer was frustrated that many people do not seem able to learn this lesson until a life is at stake. Kramer felt that people needed to learn to be sympathetic toward others before a life is at stake. However, to Kramer, it was even worse to never care about someone who is dying. Kramer felt that his doctors, Dr. Gordon and Dr. Denlon, were unsympathetic even after he was diagnosed with a terminal disease. That is why he trapped them.

Dr. Gordon's actions leading to his trap encompassed many of the problems Kramer had with the way people treat each other. Gordon used his intern during their affair. He was not sympathetic or caring toward others, especially his patients, even when they were dying. He also did not care enough about his family's problems. When asked to check his daughter's room for the "bad

---

180 Frost, S. E. *Basic Teachings of the Great Philosophers: a Survey of Their Basic Ideas.* New York: Anchor, 1989. Page 133. Print.

man" while she was trying to fall asleep, Gordon put his work first. Though he did have a bond with his daughter, he showed little concern for her safety. Had he actually checked her room, he might have discovered the man who was hiding in her closet.[181]

Dr. Denlon also showed a lack of empathy for others. For example, she approached Young with complete numbness when Young was very upset about Kramer's rough recovery from brain surgery.[182] Young was crying as she leaned over Kramer, trying to tell him something. Denlon told her coldly, "He can't hear you. He doesn't even know you're there." This showed that she lacked the ability to be sympathetic to other people.[183]

Kramer believed that the need for revenge was an especially stark manifestation of a person's inability to be understanding and sympathetic toward others. This was demonstrated through the series of tests that one of the main characters of *SAW III*, Jeff Denlon, was forced to endure.

After Jeff Denlon lost his son in a drunk driving accident, he was consumed by a desire for vengeance

---

181 Trap Index, #10A; *SAW*. Dir. James Wan. Screenplay by Leigh Whannell. Prod. Gregg Hoffman, Oren Koules, and Mark Burg. Perf. Leigh Whannell, Carey Elwes, Danny Glover. Lionsgate, 2005. DVD.

182 Trap Index, #19 & #19A; *SAW III*. Dir. Darren L. Bousman. Screenplay by Leigh Whannell and Darren L. Bousman. Prod. Gregg Hoffman, Oren Koules, Mark Burg, and James Wan. Perf. Tobin Bell, Shawnee Smith, Angus MacFadyn. Lionsgate, 2007. DVD.

183 *SAW III*. Dir. Darren L. Bousman. Screenplay by Leigh Whannell and Darren L. Bousman. Prod. Gregg Hoffman, Oren Koules, Mark Burg, and James Wan. Perf. Tobin Bell, Shawnee Smith, Angus MacFadyn. Lionsgate, 2007. DVD.

against the drunk driver who he believed had murdered his son as well as others who had failed to assure that this murderer was brought to justice. Denlon had to undergo a series of tests that were intended to teach him forgiveness. Each test presented Denlon with the opportunity to save someone whom he deemed partially or completely responsible for his pain. Each test was meant to teach him that those against whom he sought revenge were just people like him and his son. All of the people involved had special circumstances and reasons for doing what they did. Denlon needed to learn to forgive them for their mistakes and cherish their lives, even though they were responsible for the death of his son or the failure of the drunken driver to suffer appropriate consequences. [184]

If Denlon did not learn to cherish their lives, it would only bring him more pain. If Denlon carried out his revenge, his pain would not stop, but instead would get worse. During Denlon's tests, he encountered the judge who sentenced his son's murderer very lightly. After seeing how much pain this had caused Denlon, the judge said, "No sentence I gave him—not 500 years, not even ten, nothing, will take your pain away. And vengeance doesn't solve anything. It only makes the pain

---

184 Trap Index, #19B; *SAW III*. Dir. Darren L. Bousman. Screenplay by Leigh Whannell and Darren L. Bousman. Prod. Gregg Hoffman, Oren Koules, Mark Burg, and James Wan. Perf. Tobin Bell, Shawnee Smith, Angus MacFadyn. Lionsgate, 2007. DVD.; *SAW IV*. Dir. Darren L. Bousman. Screenplay by Patrick Melton and Marcus Dunstan. Prod. Gregg Hoffman, Oren Koules, Mark Burg, James Wan, and Leigh Whannell. Perf. Tobin Bell, Scott Patterson, Luis Ferreiera. Lionsgate, 2008. DVD.

greater."[185] Denlon needed to learn to be sympathetic and understanding toward those who had wronged him in order for the pain to go away.

In the end, both Kramer and the judge were correct. In the final test of the series, Denlon was given the chance to take his revenge upon Kramer. Denlon did not know that Kramer's heart rate monitor was connected to a device that was worn by Denlon's wife. Denlon did not realize that if he killed Kramer, the device would then kill his wife. Denlon took revenge, killing Kramer, even though he had been repeatedly warned that the consequences would be deadly.[186] This was a graphic and tragic illustration of the ultimate connection that Kramer saw between seeking revenge and causing more pain.

Shaping One's Life

Kramer believed that anyone could follow any of the eight ways to happiness at any time, no matter what was happening in their life, good or bad. There is an important conversation in the series that demonstrates this.

When Detective Hoffman and his colleague, Lieutenant Daniel Rigg, discovered the body of another colleague, Detective Alison Kerry, they found the

185 *SAW III*. Dir. Darren L. Bousman. Screenplay by Leigh Whannell and Darren L. Bousman. Prod. Gregg Hoffman, Oren Koules, Mark Burg, and James Wan. Perf. Tobin Bell, Shawnee Smith, Angus MacFadyn. Lionsgate, 2007. DVD.

186 *SAW III*. Dir. Darren L. Bousman. Screenplay by Leigh Whannell and Darren L. Bousman. Prod. Gregg Hoffman, Oren Koules, Mark Burg, and James Wan. Perf. Tobin Bell, Shawnee Smith, Angus MacFadyn. Lionsgate, 2007. DVD.

words "cherish your life" written on the wall above her corpse.[187] This was a warning to Rigg that, if he did not change his ways, he would soon be tested for the same type of obsessive behavior as Kerry. Hoffman and Rigg then had the following discussion, which occurred before anyone knew that Hoffman was working as Kramer's accomplice:[188]

"I didn't see it happening like this. Why the hell do we still do it?" asked Hoffman.

"It's in our nature to save people. It's what we do," replied Rigg, unknowingly sharing his obsession with the man who would soon set up the trap to test it.

"Right—cherish your life," said Hoffman, attempting to give Rigg a further warning. If Rigg had learned to cherish his life and stop obsessing, he would not have been put in a trap.

"What?" asked Rigg, clearly not understanding that he was being warned.

"The fucking motto. We're supposed to cherish our lives," said Hoffman, giving him yet another, more blatant warning.

"Well, how the hell are we supposed to do that when this is our life?" asked Rigg, showing his continued

---

187 Trap Index #17; *SAW IV*. Dir. Darren L. Bousman. Screenplay by Patrick Melton and Marcus Dunstan. Prod. Gregg Hoffman, Oren Koules, Mark Burg, James Wan, and Leigh Whannell. Perf. Tobin Bell, Scott Patterson, Luis Ferreiera. Lionsgate, 2008. DVD.

188 *SAW IV*. Dir. Darren L. Bousman. Screenplay by Patrick Melton and Marcus Dunstan. Prod. Gregg Hoffman, Oren Koules, Mark Burg, James Wan, and Leigh Whannell. Perf. Tobin Bell, Scott Patterson, Luis Ferreiera. Lionsgate, 2008. DVD.

inability to understand, which ultimately became the cause of his death.

"We chose this. You go home," replied Hoffman, going so far as to give him advice on how to survive his trap, but Rigg still did not listen.

This conversation is important because it expresses the idea that there is always a way to improve one's life. A number of traps express this same idea. Kramer recognized that people commonly seem to become overwhelmed by their problems to the point that they affect the quality of their lives. It was important to Kramer that people learn that there is always a way to rebuild life when things get bad.

The eight ways to happiness can help people rebuild their lives. If one is unable to follow Kramer's eight-fold path, then they may never learn to cherish their life until they are dying. Kramer saw that many people had difficulty appreciating life until they were faced with death. That is why he said, "the knowledge of death changes everything."[189] The knowledge of death causes one to savor everything from a cup of water to a walk in the park. Kramer's goal was to teach people to appreciate these things well before they were dying—before it was too late.

Will to Survive

Kramer believed that it is very important for people to understand their will to survive. Kramer considered

189 *SAW II*. Dir. Darren L. Bousman. Screenplay by Leigh Whannell and Darren L. Bousman. Prod. Gregg Hoffman, Oren Koules, Mark Burg, and James Wan. Perf. Donnie Wahlberg, Beverley Mitchell, Franky G. Lionsgate, 2006. DVD.

the will to live "the most important human element of all."[190] Arthur Schopenhauer was a philosopher who believed in the importance of human will and that the will exists in everything. In Schopenhauer's view, the will is "fundamental to the universe."[191]

Survival of the Fittest. Both Kramer and Schopenhauer recognized that survival of the fittest was at the core of human nature, that it is what guided people who lived in a natural state. However, Schopenhauer considered the will to be the cause of everything evil, while Kramer believed that the will to survive is an instinct that we must listen to.[192] Kramer did not believe that the will to live is a cause of evil. Kramer believed that the will to survive is an instinct that must be recognized and used to improve one's life.

Kramer believed that people today have lost their instinct to fight for their lives because they generally are not faced with life-threatening situations and death as much as people of earlier times were. He believed that "survival of the fittest no longer applies on this planet." This is why he cut a jigsaw piece out of each test subject who died, which explains his nickname. "The jigsaw piece I cut from my subjects was only ever meant to be a symbol that that subject was missing

---

190 *SAW VI.* Dir. Kevin Greutert. Screenplay by Patrick Melton and Marcus Dunstan. Prod. Gregg Hoffman, Oren Koules, Mark Burg, James Wan, and Leigh Whannell. Perf. Tobin Bell, Costas Mandylor, Mark Rolston. Lions Gate, 2010. DVD.

191 Frost, S. E. *Basic Teachings of the Great Philosophers: a Survey of Their Basic Ideas.* New York: Anchor, 1989. Page 96. Print.

192 Frost, S. E. *Basic Teachings of the Great Philosophers: a Survey of Their Basic Ideas.* New York: Anchor, 1989. Page 96. Print.

something—a vital piece of the human puzzle—the survival instinct."[193]

There are similarities between Schopenhauer's philosophy and Kramer's philosophy because they both agreed that sympathy and pity are important to morality. However, Schopenhauer believed that fighting against the will to survive is how one gets to a state of sympathy and morality, while Kramer believed the opposite.[194] Kramer believed that people should learn to listen to their will to survive and still find a way to be sympathetic and understanding toward others. Unlike Schopenhauer, Kramer did not believe that one had to give up the will to survive in order to be sympathetic toward others.

Utilitarianism. Part of Kramer's philosophy, as shown in the group traps, is a type of utilitarianism. The basic idea of utilitarianism is that the good is what produces "the greatest good of the greatest number."[195] Sometimes one may have to sacrifice something of oneself to promote this greatest good, but ultimately it will be worth the sacrifice.[196] In utilitarian ethics, the consequences of

193 *SAW II*. Dir. Darren L. Bousman. Screenplay by Leigh Whannell and Darren L. Bousman. Prod. Gregg Hoffman, Oren Koules, Mark Burg, and James Wan. Perf. Donnie Wahlberg, Beverley Mitchell, Franky G. Lionsgate, 2006. DVD.

194 Frost, S. E. *Basic Teachings of the Great Philosophers: a Survey of Their Basic Ideas.* New York: Anchor, 1989. Page 96. Print.

195 Frost, S. E. *Basic Teachings of the Great Philosophers: a Survey of Their Basic Ideas.* New York: Anchor, 1989. Page 97. Print.

196 Solomon, Robert C. *Introducing Philosophy.* Ninth ed. New York: Oxford UP, 2008. Page 514. Print.

actions are very important because the best actions will bring about the best results for the group.[197]

John Stuart Mill believed that good actions differ in quality, while Jeremy Bentham did not differentiate between qualities.[198] Kramer's philosophy is more similar to Mill's than Bentham's. This is because utilitarianism did not necessarily distinguish between happiness and pleasure, but Kramer did.[199] As discussed before, Kramer differentiated between qualities of things that make us feel happy and things that actually make us happy.

Kramer's traps did not focus only on the good of the group. They also focused on the good of each individual. This is similar to the thinking of William James and John Dewey, who taught that the individual is not just a means to an end, where the end is to serve the group. To James and Dewey, as well as Kramer, the greatest good serves both the individual and the group.[200]

One of Kramer's group traps provides an example of this in Kramer's work. Five people were put through a series of tests in which they had to work together, suffering minor discomfort, so they so all could survive.[201]

197 Frost, S. E. *Basic Teachings of the Great Philosophers: a Survey of Their Basic Ideas.* New York: Anchor, 1989. Page 97. Print.

198 Frost, S. E. *Basic Teachings of the Great Philosophers: a Survey of Their Basic Ideas.* New York: Anchor, 1989. Page 97. Print.

199 Solomon, Robert C. *Introducing Philosophy.* Ninth ed. New York: Oxford UP, 2008. Page 514. Print.

200 Frost, S. E. *Basic Teachings of the Great Philosophers: a Survey of Their Basic Ideas.* New York: Anchor, 1989. Page 98. Print.

201 Trap Index, #22; *SAW V.* Dir. David Hackl. Screenplay by Patrick Melton and Marcus Dunstan. Prod. Gregg Hoffman, Oren Koules, Mark Burg, James Wan, and Leigh Whannell. Perf. Scott Patterson, Costas Mandylor, Tobin Bell. Lionsgate, 2009. DVD.

In each test, they had to sacrifice some comfort in order to cause "the greatest good for the greatest number."[202]

Kramer made this trap reflect how he thought the balance between survival of the fittest and sympathy towards others should work. The fittest subjects, the only two to survive, were the two who figured out that they had to work together to survive. So in a sense, utilitarianism was the way Kramer resolved his conflict between survival of the fittest and having sympathy for others. He believed the truly fit would realize that their survival is dependent on the group. This is why in the last part of the test, he said, "This journey has been one of discovery and hopefully you've discovered that the whole is greater than the sum of its parts."[203]

This is how Kramer's ethical lessons bridged the gap and solved the problems raised by Schopenhauer's philosophy. Both Schopenhauer and Kramer wanted people to learn "that every individual is actually part of the whole—the universal will. The one against whom we struggle is actually part of the whole of which we are also members. When we reach this understanding, we will stop struggling and will develop sympathetic understanding."[204]

---

202 Solomon, Robert C. *Introducing Philosophy.* Ninth ed. New York: Oxford UP, 2008. Page 514. Print.

203 *SAW V.* Dir. David Hackl. Screenplay by Patrick Melton and Marcus Dunstan. Prod. Gregg Hoffman, Oren Koules, Mark Burg, James Wan, and Leigh Whannell. Perf. Scott Patterson, Costas Mandylor, Tobin Bell. Lionsgate, 2009. DVD.

204 Frost, S. E. *Basic Teachings of the Great Philosophers: a Survey of Their Basic Ideas.* New York: Anchor, 1989. Page 96. Print.

Chapter 5:

CONCLUSION

K ramer's primary messages about the value of life were sound moral concepts based on longstanding philosophical themes, and Kramer's objective of enlightening people who did not appreciate their lives was commendable. Kramer's cruel methods, however, did not work and are impossible to justify. The more interesting and important question is whether one can justify the delivery of valuable lessons about morality through horror movies such as the *SAW* series.

Kramer's Intentions

A detective provided a fair characterization of Kramer's work: "Putting a gun to someone's head and forcing them to pull the trigger is still murder."[205] In most systems of ethics, Kramer's actions would be considered unethical, notwithstanding his good intentions. In some ethical systems, however, Kramer's good intentions may have made his actions slightly more acceptable, but not completely justifiable.

---

205 *SAW II*. Dir. Darren L. Bousman. Screenplay by Leigh Whannell and Darren L. Bousman. Prod. Gregg Hoffman, Oren Koules, Mark Burg, and James Wan. Perf. Donnie Wahlberg, Beverley Mitchell, Franky G. Lionsgate, 2006. DVD.

Kantian ethics is an example of a system that determines morality based upon intention. For Kant, and other philosophers such as Wittgenstein, the consequences of an action do not matter.[206] Therefore, the fact that most of Kramer's test subjects died should not matter in assessing his morality. However, Kant also believed that someone's morality can be judged by whether they were intending to promote happiness or pain.[207] It is not clear how to apply this concept to Kramer because he promoted pain that he hoped would lead to happiness. On the other hand, the verdict on Detective Hoffman is clear. As a pure killer, he promoted only pain, and his actions were obviously immoral.

The ethics of Herbert Spencer also provide a partial justification of Kramer's actions. Spencer differentiates between actions that are "absolutely right" and actions that are "relatively right." Absolutely right actions are good in the moment and produce goodness in the future, while relatively right actions produce only goodness in the future.[208] Kramer's actions may be considered to be relatively right, since they were intended to and sometimes did produce a better future. However, Spencer also believed that one should aim for absolutely right actions.[209] So according to this ethical

---

206 Melchert, Norman. *The Great Conversation.* Fifth ed. 2 Vols. New York: Oxford UP, 2007. Page 610. Print.

207 Frost, S. E. *Basic Teachings of the Great Philosophers: a Survey of Their Basic Ideas.* New York: Anchor, 1989. Pages 94-95. Print.

208 Frost, S. E. *Basic Teachings of the Great Philosophers: a Survey of Their Basic Ideas.* New York: Anchor, 1989. Page 98. Print.

209 Frost, S. E. *Basic Teachings of the Great Philosophers: a Survey of Their Basic Ideas.* New York: Anchor, 1989. Page 98. Print.

system, what Kramer did might have had some relative merit, but did not achieve the ultimate goal of absolute right.

The fact that Kramer had good intentions may complicate the assessment of his morality, but in the end most philosophers would conclude that Kramer's traps were unethical. However, this complexity is what makes Kramer far more interesting and, therefore, more difficult to judge than the typical horror movie serial killer. James Wan, the director of the first movie in the series, explained this well:

> *He's not actually punishing people for their sins. He's not one of those killers. He's a guy who wants to help you appreciate life and not take it for granted. I think that's what sets him different to a lot of other movie serial killers. His motive is very different. He wants to help people out. If you can survive one of his games, . . . he's happy for that. He wants you to survive his games [because] . . . if you make it out of one of his games alive then he believes . . . you'll be a better person.*[210]

Kramer's Methods

Wan was not just describing Kramer's intentions; he was also characterizing his methods. Wan's quote makes clear that he viewed Kramer more as a well-intentioned teacher than as a vigilante trying to punish people for their sins. Kramer did, however, act like a vigilante in one

---

210 *Hacking Away At SAW*. Prod. Mark Atkinson and Kelly L. Pancho. Lions Gate, 2005. DVD.

important sense: he alone decided who should be tested in his traps. Moreover, his range of test subjects extended well beyond what most people would consider criminals deserving of punishment.

Vigilantism is widely considered to be wrong. According to many different philosophers, one enters society in order to be protected. Thomas Hobbes, like many others, believed that "in the state of nature, human beings are governed by their egoistic passions, their endeavor to ensure their own happiness." To Hobbes, this results in a war in which everyone is an enemy.[211] Humans must band together to protect each other and to feel safe. The government and society came together because of the human need to protect each other from themselves.[212] When one decides to take the law into their own hands by punishing those who they deem worthy of punishment, the foundation on which society and government were originally built is destroyed.

Similarly, John Locke wrote that once someone is a part of society, they give up their ability to punish someone who has done wrong or has gone "against the laws of nature."[213] A vigilante tears down the structure of society and creates an unsafe situation similar to the dangerous state of nature described by Hobbes.

Some philosophers have advocated for the right of individuals to take the law into their own hands in

---

211 Melchert, Norman. *The Great Conversation.* Fifth ed. 2 Vols. New York: Oxford UP, 2007. Page 369. Print.

212 Frost, S. E. *Basic Teachings of the Great Philosophers: a Survey of Their Basic Ideas.* New York: Anchor, 1989. Pages 176. Print.

213 Arthur, John, and William H. Shaw. *Social and Political Philosophy.* Englewood Cliffs, NJ: Prentice Hall, 1992. 500. Print.

certain circumstances, but this is usually limited to non-violent civil disobedience. One of the most well known advocates of civil disobedience was Henry David Thoreau, who argued that "for a person to obey the laws of a government which behaves unjustly would be the same as his behaving unjustly."[214] This could justify the actions of Kramer or Hoffman to the extent that they did a better job than the police of administering justice to dangerous criminals. It does not, however, justify Kramer's trapping of people who did not cherish their lives but did not commit actual crimes.

Many people believe that true criminals deserve some form of punishment, but few believe that those who do not appreciate their lives should be punished for that. This gets at the heart of why most philosophers believe that vigilantism is wrong. The choice of who deserves punishment, especially capital punishment, must be determined by consensus and legal process, not by individuals. Vigilantism is wrong because one individual's opinion should never be sufficient to determine life or death for another.

Value of the *SAW* Series

Despite his good intentions, Kramer's vigilantism and intentional infliction of pain were wrong and unjustifiable. With that in mind, one may ask whether there is any value to the *SAW* movies and their display of the gory consequences of Kramer's unethical behavior.

---

214 Solomon, Robert C. *Introducing Philosophy*. Ninth ed. New York: Oxford UP, 2008. Page 596 Print.

The moral of the *SAW* movies is that people should cherish their lives and the lives of others, not that people should be vigilantes or do what John Kramer did. Trying to teach morality is an admirable goal, but if any viewers were to mistake the message and imitate Kramer, that would be a terrible outcome. The movies put both their fictional subjects and their real-life viewers in uncomfortable situations in order to teach morality, but if the traps became real and people died in them, the value of the good messages would be lost.

The next question is whether it is justifiable to use gruesome imagery to impart morality. Some viewers see the *SAW* series as an exercise in gratuitous violence without redeeming value. For those who can endure the gore, however, the movies are a dramatic use of cinematography to reinforce ethical teachings. Like many stories, the *SAW* movies do have clear messages about life and morality. "That's one of the things that attracted us to the film immediately, that it was trying to say something and it did have a theme, that it did have a moral message despite . . . the smears of blood throughout the bathroom and everywhere else," said Gregg Hoffman, one of the producers.[215] "I like to think of the story as a very twisted morality tale," said Carey Elwes, the actor who played Dr. Gordon.[216]

For centuries, humans have used stories to distinguish wrong from right. Examples of these are Aesop's Fables and Grimm's Fairytales, which were

---

215 *Hacking Away At SAW.* Prod. Mark Atkinson and Kelly L. Pancho. Lions Gate, 2005. DVD.

216 *Hacking Away At SAW.* Prod. Mark Atkinson and Kelly L. Pancho. Lions Gate, 2005. DVD.

written to teach children lessons about bad behavior. Fables and fairy tales are often very frightening and depict extremely grisly images, but that is what makes them memorable. Their gruesomeness not only gives voice to our innermost nightmares, but also adds shock value to underscore each story's moral.

Like many fables and fairy tales, the *SAW* movies are horror stories that teach morality. They are Grimm's Fairytales for adults living today. They show examples of how people should not live and they do this with violent images. The movies do not need to be so violent to make their point, but if they were not, the messages would not be as vivid and unforgettable.

Unlike folktales of old, the *SAW* movies use modern film techniques to graphically depict gruesome scenes. In doing so, *SAW* films attain the cutting edge of folklore, for they become metaphysical representations of their stories. John Kramer's traps were fictional, but the *SAW* movies themselves are real-life traps for their viewers. Instead of "How much blood will you shed to stay alive?" it is "How much bloodshed will you watch to learn the value of life?"

INDEX

INDEX

Sophism, 38-39
Spencer, Herbert, 78
Stoicism, 43, 65-66

T

Tapp, David, 62
Thoreau, Henry David, 81
Thrasymachus, 38
Transcendence, 54
Tuck, Jill, 19-20, 24, 27, 30, 34

U

Urban Renewal Group, 12
Utilitarianism, 74-76

V

Vigilantism, 79-82

W

Wan, James, 79
Will to survive, 1, 2, 25, 34, 36, 73-74
Wittgenstein, Ludwig, 42-43, 78

Y

Yoruba Philosophy, 44-45
Young, Amanda, 24-28, 31-32, 66, 68

TRAP INDEX

This index presents the details of each trap in the *SAW* films: the name of the trap, the movie in which it appeared, who set up the trap, who was the test subject, why the test subject was trapped, a description of the trap, what the test subject's options were, the result, and my comments. The names of the traps may or may not match the "official" name found on the *SAW* website or any other source; they represent my assessment of the best name for each trap, taking into account the instructional audio or video tape for the trap.

All traps except one are listed in chronological order, based on when the trap started, not when it ended. It was necessary to choose a timing convention because some traps overlap other traps, and some traps are broader or longer traps that encompass one or more narrower or shorter traps. The one trap of unknown timing is presented at the end of the index.

Be forewarned: many of the gory details of the traps, which were omitted from the body of the book, are presented here.

1. <u>**Knife Chair**</u>

Movie:	*SAW IV*
Set Up:	John Kramer
Subject:	Cecil Adams
Reason:	Adams was a drug abuser, hustler and thief who played roulette with the lives of others and preyed on the kindness of others to fuel his addiction. His greed eventually caused Jill Tuck's miscarriage.
Description:	Adams was seated in a chair with restraints on his wrists and legs, which were causing him to bleed. In front of his face were a group of knives with the blades facing Adams. The knives were attached to a lever that, if pushed far enough, would release the restraints.
Success:	Adams had to push his face forward into the knives, maiming his face, until the restraints on his wrists and legs were released.
Failure:	Adams would bleed to death.
Result:	Success
Comments:	Although Kramer's first test subject was the man who killed his unborn son, Kramer convinced himself that he was not trapping Adams out of a desire for revenge. Instead, Kramer believed that he could help Adams by trapping him. Kramer believed that Adams put himself in this trap by being an immoral criminal who did not appreciate life.

Kramer believed that it was his duty to give Adams a "tool" to reclaim his life and help him "discard the devices that have so corrupted [his] soul." Kramer wanted Adams to see himself for who he really was, to have the ugliness inside him come out into the open, and to make his face as ugly as his soul. However, the tragic and warped flaw in Kramer's technique showed up right away in this first trap. Adams could not survive without gruesome consequences, making it extremely difficult for him to have learned from the experience. Kramer showed that he understood this risk because he set up a second trap for Adams (Trap #2) just in case this first trap left Adams vengeful and enraged.

2. **<u>Razor Wire I</u>**

Movie:	*SAW IV*
Set Up:	John Kramer
Subject:	Cecil Adams
Reason:	Adams might survive his first trap (Trap #1) and attack Kramer.
Description:	Adams stood facing Kramer, unaware that there was a tangled mass of razor wire behind Kramer.
Success:	Adams had to leave Kramer's lair without trying to harm him.
Failure:	Adams would attempt to attack Kramer and end up falling into the razor wire and bleeding to death.
Result:	Failure
Comments:	Passing his first test (Trap #1) showed that Adams had the will to live, but he then showed that he did not learn anything from the experience. He was consumed by anger, which cost him any chance of gaining insight from the test. As Adams struggled to stand after escaping the first trap, he growled menacingly at Kramer, "You're dead! You're fucking dead! Fucking dead!" Adams then charged at Kramer, but Kramer stepped aside and Adams fell into the razor wire. To Kramer, this was Adams' fault; he deserved to die because he did not learn to appreciate life. This trap presumably was Kramer's inspiration for the iconic Razor Wire II trap (Trap #5).

3. **The Pendulum**

Movie:	*SAW V*
Set Up:	Detective Mark Hoffman
Subject:	Seth Baxter
Reason:	Baxter murdered Hoffman's sister (and only relative) by slitting her throat, but due to a legal technicality, served only five years of what should have been a life sentence.
Description:	Baxter was lying on a metal slab with a razor sharp pendulum swinging above his abdomen and two devices on either side of him at arm's length. The pendulum lowered incrementally as time passed.
Result:	Unwinnable. Baxter was told that if he inserted his hands into the two devices, his hands would be crushed and his restraints would be released. Baxter did this, but the restraints were not released and he was slowly sliced in half by the pendulum.
Comments:	This was Hoffman's way of getting revenge and delivering justice. Hoffman wanted Baxter to feel helpless because Baxter had bestowed that same feeling onto others. Hoffman also wanted Baxter to be forced to destroy the very instruments he had used to kill: his hands. Ironically, in setting up this unwinnable trap, Hoffman committed the very same crime as Baxter.

4. <u>**Shotgun Trigger**</u>

Movie:	*SAW V*
Set Up:	John Kramer
Subject:	Detective Mark Hoffman
Reason:	Hoffman murdered Seth Baxter (Trap #3) and made it look like one of Kramer's traps.
Description:	Hoffman was sitting in a chair with his wrists bound by rope. The rope was connected to a double-barrel shotgun that was pointed right at his head. There was a mirror across from Hoffman.
Option 1:	Hoffman could turn Kramer in, causing Kramer to turn in evidence against Hoffman.
Option 2:	Hoffman could become Kramer's accomplice.
Result:	Option 2
Comments:	Kramer positioned the mirror in front of Hoffman because Kramer wanted Hoffman to see himself clearly. Kramer had the shotgun pointing at Hoffman's head because Kramer wanted Hoffman to think very carefully about his next decision. Although the shotgun appeared to be loaded, it was not, as Hoffman eventually learned. This may have been an attempt by Kramer to gain Hoffman's trust by letting him know that Kramer did not intend to kill him. However, Kramer must have

been wary of Hoffman right from the start. This trap was the first of Kramer's ongoing series of traps for Hoffman that would take place throughout their relationship, endure beyond Kramer's death, and ultimately end in failure and death for Hoffman.

5. <u>Razor Wire II</u>

Movie: *SAW*

Set Up: John Kramer and Detective Mark Hoffman

Subject: Paul Leahy

Reason: Leahy was a perfectly healthy, apparently sane, middle class male, yet a month before this trap, he ran a straight razor across his wrists and then continued to cut himself until the night he was kidnapped.

Description: Leahy was in a room with a single door. His path to the door was blocked by a tangled mass of razor wire. A device would permanently seal the room when time expired.

Success: Leahy had to navigate through the razor wire and exit the room before time expired.

Failure:
  (1) Leahy would bleed to death trying to escape.
  (2) Leahy would fail to escape in time and be sealed in the room until he died.
  (3) Leahy would do nothing and bleed to death from inactivity.

Result: Failure #1

Comments: Kramer was assessing whether Leahy truly wanted to die or if he just wanted attention. If Leahy truly wanted to die, he could have done nothing or he could have intentionally killed himself. He did neither, but was still unable to escape. This is an example of an ill-conceived trap because there was a high risk of dying while trying to escape. This also is an example of a test subject whom many people would not consider sufficiently evil or flawed to be put in a life-threatening trap. Nevertheless, this trap produced one of the most iconic lines of the *SAW* series when Kramer asked Leahy in the instructional tape: "How much blood will you shed to stay alive?"

6. **<u>Flammable Substance</u>**

    Movie: *SAW*

    Set Up: John Kramer and Detective Mark Hoffman

    Subject: Mark Rodriguez Wilson

    Reason: Wilson lied to his employer and others, claiming to be sick, so that he could go on paid long-term medical leave.

    Description: Wilson was in a dark room with broken glass all over the floor. He had been injected with a slow acting poison. He was naked with a flammable substance smeared all over his body. There was a safe in front of him that contained an antidote for the poison, and there were numbers written on the walls. There was an unlit candle and matches on the safe.

    Success: Wilson had to use the matches to light the candle, then use the candle to read the numbers on the walls, then use the numbers to open the safe, and then retrieve the antidote for the poison from the safe, while simultaneously navigating across the broken glass on the floor and being careful not to ignite the flammable substance smeared on this body.

    Failure: (1) Wilson would burn to death because the flammable substance smeared on his body would ignite.

                 (2) Wilson would die from the poison.

Result: Failure #1

Comments: Kramer wanted to put Wilson's claimed
illness to the test. The threat of burning
to death was symbolic of all the people
Wilson had "burned" with his pretenses.
This is another example of a test subject
whom many people would not deem
sufficiently evil or flawed to be put in a
life-threatening trap. It is also another
example of an ill-conceived trap that was
very difficult to escape.

7. <u>**Reverse Bear Trap I**</u>

Movie:	*SAW*
Set Up:	John Kramer
Subject:	Amanda Young
Reason:	Young was a drug abuser.

Description: Young was seated in a chair and had a device on her head that was hooked into her upper and lower jaw. There was a timer on the device that would start if Young left her chair. There was man lying on the floor that appeared to be dead but was alive.

Success: Young had to cut a key out of the stomach of the man lying on the floor and use it to unlock the device on her head before time expired.

Failure: (1) Young could do nothing and remain in the room until she starved to death.

(2) Young could leave her chair, starting the timer, but then fail to retrieve the key from the man's stomach before time expired, resulting in her jaw being ripped open by the device, killing her.

Result: Success

Comments: Kramer and Young had a complex relationship. This was the first of three traps that Kramer set for Young. After escaping this trap, Young felt that the experience helped her learn to appreciate her life. She then became Kramer's accomplice. The man on the floor had to be killed in order for Young to escape the trap. Presumably Kramer judged him to be guilty and unsalvageable, but the reasons for this are not provided in the film.

8. **<u>Drill Chair</u>**

Movie:	*SAW*
Set Up:	John Kramer
Subjects:	(1) Detective David Tapp
	(2) Detective Steven Sing
Reason:	Tapp was so obsessed with solving the Jigsaw case that Kramer wanted to test what mattered to him more— apprehending Kramer or saving the life of an apparently innocent man.
Description:	Tapp and Sing had Kramer at gunpoint in his lair. Jeff Ridenhaur was in the lair, strapped to a chair, with drills on either side of his neck.
Success:	Tapp and Sing had to rescue Ridenhaur by finding the key that would allow them to stop the drills from penetrating Ridenhaur's neck. In doing so, they would give Kramer time to escape.
Failure:	(1) Tapp and Sing could apprehend Kramer and let Ridenhaur die.
	(2) Tapp and Sing could have taken too much time trying to rescue Ridenhaur, resulting in his death.
Result:	Success. Sing fired his gun at the drills, stopping them and saving Ridenhaur. Tapp attempted to apprehend Kramer, but Kramer used a weapon to wound Tapp and escaped.
Comments:	Before the game started, Kramer told Ridenhaur not to cry, explaining that

Kramer had given Ridenhaur's life a purpose. Kramer wanted Ridenhaur to know that he was a test subject for something greater than himself—a game that would show just how far a police detective would go in order to catch a criminal. Kramer later asked Tapp and Sing: "What's more important to you, officer? Arresting me or the life of another human being?"

9. <u>Shotgun Hallway</u>

Movie: *SAW*

Set Up: John Kramer

Subject: Anyone who tried to apprehend Kramer. As it happened, Detective Steven Sing became the test subject.

Reason: This was a booby trap for anyone who pursued Kramer further into his lair.

Description: At the end of a hallway was a tripwire. The tripwire was connected to four double-barreled shotguns that hung from the ceiling at the end of the hall.

Success:
(1) Sing had to stop pursuing Kramer and tend to Tapp, who was wounded.
(2) Sing had to be more careful and check his surroundings for booby traps.

Failure: Sing would chase Kramer, neglect to notice the tripwire, and get shot in the head by the four double-barreled shotguns.

Result: Failure

Comments: This trap showed how prepared Kramer was for an invasion of his lair. Not only had he set up a distraction trap, but he also had set up dangerous booby traps. As Sing chased after Kramer with a shotgun, it was as if Kramer were saying, "You have one shotgun? Well I have four."

10. <u>Bathroom Trap I</u>

    Movie: *SAW*

    Set Up: John Kramer and Amanda Young

    Description: This involved a series of interconnected traps for Zep Hindle (Part A), Adam Faulkner (Part B), and Dr. Lawrence Gordon (Part C).

A. <u>Mother and Child</u>

    Subject: Zep Hindle

    Reason: Hindle was a hospital orderly who let people walk all over him and never took charge of his life.

    Description: Hindle had been injected with a slow acting poison. He was instructed to and did tie up Dr. Lawrence Gordon's wife, Alison, and daughter, Diana, at their home. Hindle was monitoring the other two parts of this trap by viewing Adam Faulkner (Part B) and Dr. Gordon (Part C) by video camera.

    Success: Hindle had to kill Dr. Gordon and his wife and daughter if Dr. Gordon failed his test (Part C), in which case Hindle would receive the antidote for the poison.

    Failure: Hindle would fail or refuse to kill the Gordons, in which case he would die from the poison.

    Result: Failure

Comments: Hindle was finally given the ability to take action, but failed his test mostly due to his own incompetence. Alison and Diana Gordon escaped due to the weak material Hindle used to tie them up. In the end, Hindle was murdered by Adam Faulkner (Part B) because he assumed that Faulkner was dead, without being careful and checking for a pulse.

B. Hacksaw

Subject: Adam Faulkner

Reason: Faulkner never truly lived; he "simply sat in the shadows watching others live out their lives." He approached most of his life with only anger and apathy. He made money from clients who hired him to stalk others and take pictures of them. His disregard for other people made him perfect for this job. Moreover, he seemed to care as little about his own well being as he did about anyone else's.

Description: Faulkner was in a decrepit bathroom. His ankle was shackled by chain to a pipe. He found a hacksaw in a nearby toilet, but the hacksaw could not cut the chain.

Success: Faulkner had to escape from his ankle shackle, presumably by using the hacksaw to cut off his foot, and leave the bathroom before Dr. Gordon killed him (Part C) or time expired.

Failure: (1) Faulkner could be killed by Dr. Gordon.

(2) Faulkner could have done nothing, in which case he would be left to die in the bathroom.

(3) Faulkner could have attempted to escape after three hours by finding some way to remove the shackle, but he would not have been able to leave the bathroom because Kramer locked the door from the outside.

Result: Failure #2

Comments: Kramer considered this trap to be Faulkner's wake-up call. At the beginning of the instructional tape, Kramer said, "Rise and shine, Adam." Kramer then asked Faulkner, "But what do voyeurs see when they look in the mirror?" This question implied that Faulkner was spending so much time taking pictures and looking at other people, that he was not looking at himself clearly. Kramer also wanted to test how far Faulkner's apathy went. Would he let himself die because he cared so little for his own life?

C. <u>Kill Adam</u>

Subject: Dr. Lawrence Gordon

Reason: Gordon was an oncologist. Most days of his working life he had given people the news that they were going to die soon, and he did this in a cold and uncaring way. Gordon was almost as cold and uncaring when it came to his family. He cheated on his wife and always put his work before his family.

Description: Gordon was in the same bathroom as Faulkner. His ankle was shackled by chain to a pipe on the other side of the bathroom. Faulkner found a second hacksaw and tossed it to Gordon.

Success: In order to save his wife and daughter, Gordon had to find a way to kill Faulkner.

Failure: Gordon would fail or refuse to kill Faulkner, in which case Zep Hindle (Part A) would kill Dr. Gordon and his wife and daughter.

Result: Success—although Gordon did not kill Faulkner, he did manage to escape the bathroom by cutting off his foot with the hacksaw. After crawling out of the bathroom, he cauterized his ankle on a hot pipe in the hallway.

Comments: This test was also a wake-up call. Kramer wanted to test whether Gordon could deliver the news of death so coldly when he himself was the agent of death.

11. <u>Nerve Gas House</u>

Movie:	SAW II
Set Up:	John Kramer and Detective Mark Hoffman
Reason:	All of the test subjects were criminals who engaged in antisocial behavior without regard to the detrimental effects on others. Their common bond was that they all were framed and arrested by Detective Eric Mathews, who had planted the evidence for their arrests.
Subjects:	(1) Amanda Young

                Specific

                Reason: Beginning shortly after she completed her initial test (Trap #7), Young had been cutting her wrists.

                Specific

                Test: Wrist Cutter may have been intended for Young, but she did not become the test subject for it.

        (2) Daniel Mathews, son of Detective Eric Mathews

                Specific

                Reason: Daniel Mathews had been stealing.

        (3) Jonas Singer

                Specific

                Reason: It is implied that Singer was involved in a gang or some type of organized crime.

(4) Laura Hunter

(5) Obi Tate

Specific Reason: For years, Tate had "burned" those around him with his lies, cons and deceits, and it was eventually revealed to the others in the house that he helped Kramer and Hoffman kidnap them.

Specific Test: Furnace

(6) Xavier Chavez

Specific Reason: Chavez was a controlling, overly aggressive, drug-dealing loner.

Specific Test: Pit of Squalor

(7) Gus Colyard

Specific Test: By happenstance, Magnum Eyehole

(8) Addison Corday

Specific Reason: Corday was a prostitute who had solicited Kramer.

Specific Test: By happenstance, Wrist Cutter

Description: The group was trapped inside a house with a deadly nerve agent in the air. Without the antidote, the nerve agent would kill them in two hours. The doors to the house were locked but would open in three hours. There were specific tests throughout the house, most providing potential access to doses of the antidote.

Success: Each test subject had to find a dose of the antidote. Working together would improve their chances for success.

Failure:
(1) A test subject would fail any of the specific tests.
(2) A test subject would be killed by another test subject.
(3) A test subject would panic or get worked up, allowing for the nerve agent to take effect quicker.
(4) A test subject would do nothing and die from the nerve agent.

Result:
(1) Young: Success
(2) Mathews: Success
(3) Singer: Failure #2
(4) Hunter: Failure #3
(5) Tate: Failure #1
(6) Chavez: Failure #2
(7) Colyard: Failure #1
(8) Corday: Failure #1

Comments: All of the test subjects had done wrong and had been wronged. Kramer felt they were redeemable if they could become less antisocial and learn to work as a group when necessary. In the instructional tape, Kramer said, "I can assure you that while your location is not important, what these walls offer for you is important: salvation."

A. Antidote Safe

Subject: All test subjects

Description: The group started out locked in a room. There was a safe in the room containing one dose of the antidote. The combination to the safe could be determined by solving a riddle.

Success: The test subjects had to work together as a group to discover the combination and open the safe to retrieve the antidote.

Failure: (1) The test subjects would fail to discover the combination.
(2) The test subjects would fail to open the safe by killing each other.

Result: Failure #2

B. Magnum Eyehole

Subject: Any test subject who tried to open the door. As it happened, Gus Colyard became the test subject.

Description: The group was still locked in one room. There was a key in the room, along with a note that read, "Do not attempt to use this key on the door to this room."

Success: The test subject had to heed the warning not to open the door.

Failure: The test subject would open the door and be shot in the eye.

Result: Failure

Comments: Despite the note and Young's additional warning to Colyard, he made a hasty decision without thinking clearly.

C. Furnace

Subject: Obi Tate

Description: There was a furnace device in front of Tate that contained two doses of the antidote. Retrieving the first dose was simple. Retrieving the second dose would cause a fire to start in the device, but there was a knob that could be reached to put out the fire.

Success: Tate had to crawl into the furnace, retrieve the first antidote for himself, and retrieve the second antidote for another test subject. Retrieving the second antidote would cause the fire to start and Tate would have to reach over the fire and turn the knob to put it out.

Failure: (1) Tate would retrieve only the first antidote for himself.

(2) Tate would try to retrieve the second antidote but fail to put out the fire, resulting in him burning to death.

Result: Failure #2

Comments: This was Tate's chance to redeem his life. He could atone for the games he had played with others by playing and winning one of Kramer's games. Retrieving the second dose of antidote meant putting himself at risk to save someone else, something that he ordinarily would not do.

D. Pit of Squalor

Subject: Xavier Chavez

Description: There was a large pit of uncapped syringes in the center of the room and a door on the other side of the pit. A timer started when the group entered the room.

Success: Chavez had to get in the needle pit and find the key to unlock the door, behind which was a dose of the antidote, before time expired.

Failure: Chavez would fail to find the key before time expired, resulting in the door on the other side of the room being permanently locked.

Result: Failure #1

Comments: This was a classic and ironic trap. Kramer believed Chavez had been playing a "game" as a drug dealer—"the game of offering hope to the desperate for a price." In the trap, Chavez had to crawl into a pit of squalor like those into which he had enticed or forced his customers. However, because Chavez loved to push others around, he picked up Amanda Young and dropped her into the pit. Chavez failed this test because he stalled too much in the beginning and refused to take actions for himself. After the trauma of being dropped in the pit, Young was unable to find the key before time expired.

E. **Wrist Cutter**

Subject: Any test subject who attempted to retrieve the antidote from the glass box. As it happened, Addison Corday became the test subject.

Description: There was a glass box suspended from the ceiling. In the bottom of the box, there were two hand-sized openings that were lined with razors, and there was a dose of the antidote between the two openings.

Success: The test subject had to realize that the antidote could be retrieved with one hand, using the other hand to keep the razors away.

Failure: The test subject would put both
hands into the glass box, causing
the subject's wrists to be cut and the
subject to bleed to death.

Result: Failure

Comments: This trap may have been intended for
Amanda Young, but was discovered
by Corday after the group became
separated. In desperation, Corday
did not consider her actions carefully,
as Kramer always encouraged his test
subjects to do.

12. <u>Venus Fly Trap</u>

Movie: *SAW II*

Set Up: John Kramer and Dr. Lawrence Gordon

Subject: Michael Marks

Reason: Marks' crime was similar to Adam Faulkner's crime (Trap #10B). Marks made money by spying on others. He betrayed those who trusted him and was an informant for the police.

Description: Marks woke up with a "death mask" device locked around his neck.

Success: Marks had to cut a key out of his eye and use it to unlock the device before time expired.

Failure: The device would close around Marks' head, piercing his skull with spikes and killing him.

Result: Failure

Comments: In order to survive the trap, Marks would have had to sacrifice the very faculty he relied on to snitch on others: his vision. Kramer wanted to test whether Marks was willing and able to look inward rather than outward, both literally and figuratively.

13. <u>Electrified Staircase</u>

Movie: *SAW II*

Set Up: John Kramer

Subject: Anyone who attempted to enter Kramer's lair. As it happened, several members of the police SWAT team became the test subjects.

Reason: Kramer did not want to be caught.

Description: The staircase leading to Kramer's lair was surrounded by metal fencing. There was pressure plate on one of the steps that, if stepped on, would break a person's legs and electrify the fencing.

Success: The test subjects had to turn back and abandon their effort to enter Kramer's lair.

Failure: The test subjects would proceed toward Kramer's lair.

Result: Failure

Comments: Like Shotgun Hallway (Trap #9), this was a booby trap that showed how prepared Kramer was for an invasion of his lair.

14. <u>Listen and Learn</u>

Movie: *SAW II*

Set Up: John Kramer and Detective Mark Hoffman

Subject: Detective Eric Mathews

Reason: As a police officer, Detective Mathews used excessive force and framed people in order to arrest them. As a father, he was much too hard on his son, Daniel, and even had him arrested.

Description: In an attempt to apprehend Kramer, Mathews entered Kramer's lair. Kramer told him that he needed to be patient and listen. Kramer also told Mathews that Kramer was the person who had kidnapped Daniel and was holding him in an undisclosed location.

Success: Mathews had to simply sit and talk with Kramer. If Mathews had done this for long enough, he would have found his son in a safe and secure state.

Failure: Mathews would get agitated and actively search for Daniel, resulting in Mathews being trapped again.

Result: Failure

Comments: The rules were simple and designed to test Mathews' ability to listen and be patient when necessary. If Mathews had listened to Kramer, he would have learned that his son was right there in the same room as he was for the entire duration of the test.

15. **Bathroom Trap II**

Movie: *SAW II* and *SAW III*

Set Up: Amanda Young

Subject: Detective Eric Mathews

Reason: Mathews did not care about the people he had hurt in the past and apparently did not remember all of them, even when his actions had life-altering consequences. Mathews was the reason Young was sent to prison. Young admitted to being guilty of many things, but not the drug charge Mathews had framed her for.

Description: Mathews woke up in the same bathroom used in Trap #10. His ankle was shackled by chain to a pipe in the same location where Adam Faulkner had been shackled. There was a toilet nearby. There also was a hacksaw nearby, but the hacksaw could not cut the chain.

Success: Mathews had to find a way to escape the bathroom by removing the shackle from his ankle, presumably by using the hacksaw to cut off his foot.

Failure: Mathews would be left to die in the bathroom.

Result: Success—Mathews did not use the hacksaw, but he used the toilet lid to break his foot and slide it out of the shackle.

Comments: Young used the instructional tape for this test to explain how she felt about Kramer and his work. Young explained that her life was saved on the first day Kramer tested her. In Kramer, Young had found a father, a leader, a teacher. Because of Kramer, the tables were now turned. She now had control over Mathews and claimed him as her first test subject. Now he was locked away, helpless and alone, like she had been.

16. <u>Chain Ripper</u>

Movie: *SAW III*

Set Up: Detective Mark Hoffman; designed by John Kramer

Subject: Troy

Reason: Despite all the advantages and privileges Troy was given at birth, he had returned to prison again and again, showing that he was more comfortable in chains than out of them. This game took place in a room not much bigger than the room Troy had spent most of his life in: a prison cell.

Description: Troy was chained to the walls, floor and ceiling, with metal rings going through his skin and sometimes around bones. There was a nail bomb in front of him.

Result: Unwinnable. Troy was told that he had to pull all of the chains out of his skin and off his bones before time expired and the bomb detonated. However, there were certain chains that were impossible to pull out, and the door to the room was welded shut, making escape impossible.

Comments: Kramer designed this as a symbolic test for Troy. The idea was to see how hard Troy would work to break the literal and figurative chains that bound him to a life of imprisonment. However, Hoffman thwarted Kramer's plan by making this trap unwinnable.

17. <u>Angel Trap</u>

Movie: *SAW III*

Set Up: Detective Mark Hoffman; designed by
                   John Kramer

Subject: Detective Allison Kerry

Reason: Kerry was a homicide detective who
spent her entire career among the dead,
piecing together their final moments.
She was more comfortable with cold
corpses than living humans. This game
tested her will to survive by giving her
the choice between joining her "true
family" in death or suffering great pain
to remain alive. Kerry was also obsessed
with finding Detective Eric Mathews and
this obsession had interfered with her
sleep and her quality of life.

Description: Kerry was suspended in air by a device
that was hooked into both sides of her
ribcage. There was a jar hanging in
front of her that was full of acid and
there was a key at the bottom of the jar.

Result: Unwinnable. Kerry was told that the
key would unlock the device and that
she had to reach into the jar of acid
to retrieve the key before the acid
dissolved it. However, even though she
completed this task, the device would
not unlock and her ribs were ripped out
of her chest, killing her.

Comments: Kramer believed that Kerry was good at her job because she, like her subjects, was dead—in her case, dead on the inside. Perhaps surviving a grueling game would have helped free her from her obsession with finding Mathews. However, like Chain Ripper (Trap #16), this trap was sabotaged by Hoffman making it unwinnable.

18. <u>Blind vs. Mute</u>

    Movie: *SAW IV*

    Set Up: John Kramer and Dr. Lawrence Gordon

    Subjects: (1) Art Blank

                  Reason: Blank was a lawyer who had defended many people who were clearly guilty.

            (2) Trevor

            Reason: Unknown

    Description: Blank was on one side of the room with his mouth sewn shut. Trevor was on the other side of the room with his eyes sewn shut. Both men were chained to a device in the center of the room via collar shackles around their necks. On the back of Trevor's shackle was the key that would unlock Blank's collar. Presumably, the key to unlock Trevor's collar was on the back of Blank's shackle.

    Option 1:   The subjects had to figure out how to communicate so they could work together to unlock their collars before the device to which they were chained crushed them.

    Option 2:   One of the subjects could kill the other in order to escape.

    Option 3:   Both subjects could be killed.

    Result: Option 2

    Comments: With the clear advantage of sight, Blank killed Trevor in order to escape. This effectively seems to be an unwinnable trap for Trevor, but there is no explanation of this in the film.

19. <u>Emotional Control</u>

Movie: *SAW III* and *SAW IV*

Set Up: John Kramer

Subject: Amanda Young

Reason: Young was emotionally unstable. She killed Faulkner rather than letting him suffer the consequences of failing his trap (Trap #10B), and she beat up Detective Mathews (Trap #15). Also, Kramer incorrectly believed that Young had rigged the unwinnable traps (Traps #16 and #17), even though it was Hoffman who actually had done that.

Description: Kramer made Young believe that she was overseeing two traps, one for Dr. Lynn Denlon (Part A) and the other for her husband, Jeff Denlon (Part B). Both traps took place in Jigsaw's lair. Kramer was in the final stages of his brain cancer and was together with Young and Dr. Denlon in a room in his lair that had been set up as a hospital operating room.

Success: Young had to control her emotions, refrain from interfering with Dr. Denlon's efforts to survive her trap, and let Dr. Denlon go free if she survived her trap.

Failure: (1) Young would interfere with Dr. Denlon's efforts to survive her trap.

> (2) Young would fail to let Dr. Denlon go free if she survived her trap.

Result: Failure #2

Comments: This was supposed to be Young's final test and turned out to be exactly that. Kramer wanted Young to succeed, but died believing that she failed. Young did allow Dr. Denlon to proceed with her trap (Part A), but eventually shot her because Hoffman had blackmailed Young. When Jeff Denlon completed his trap (Part B), he was led to the room where Kramer was dying. As he entered, Denlon saw Young shoot his wife and became enraged, so he shot Young. As Young was dying, Kramer explained that even though he made Young think that she was testing Jeff and Lynn Denlon, Kramer was actually testing Young. Ironically, Kramer would die never knowing that Young shot Dr. Denlon only because she had been blackmailed by Hoffman, not because she failed to control her emotions.

A. <u>Explosive Collar</u>

Movie: *SAW III*

Set Up: John Kramer, Amanda Young, and Dr. Lawrence Gordon

Subject: Dr. Lynn Denlon

Reason: Dr. Denlon was a brilliant neurosurgeon, but was so apathetic toward her patients that Kramer wondered whether she could truly care for anyone. This apathy carried over into Dr. Denlon's personal life as she cheated on her husband and over-dosed on anti-depressants.

Description: Dr. Denlon was wearing a collar with several shotgun bullets pointed at her head. This device was linked to Kramer's heart rate monitor and would go off if Kramer's heart stopped. The device was also was linked to a motion sensor and would go off if Dr. Denlon moved out of range or attempted to remove the collar.

Success: Dr. Denlon had to keep Kramer alive throughout the duration of her husband's trap (Part B).

Failure:
    (1) Dr. Denlon would let Kramer die or be unable to keep him alive.
    (2) Dr. Denlon would move out of range or attempt to remove the collar.
    (3) Dr. Denlon would kill Amanda Young, which presumably would have caused Kramer to immediately end the game by unplugging his heart-rate monitor.

Result: Success

Comments: Even though Dr. Denlon succeeded, she was later shot by Young. However, the gunshot did not kill her. She was killed when her collar exploded as a result of her husband failing his final test (Part B4).

B. Seek No Revenge

Movie: *SAW III* and *SAW IV*

Set Up: John Kramer and Detective Mark Hoffman

Subject: Jeff Denlon

Reason: The Denlons' son, Dylan, was killed by a drunk driver, Timothy Young, who was set free after a hasty, flawed trial. Jeff Denlon was unable to recover from this, becoming a shell of his former self, consumed with hatred and vengeance. He became obsessed with Dylan's possessions and sought violent revenge against Timothy Young and those who were involved in the trial. Denlon also began neglecting his daughter, Corbett.

Description: Denlon was trapped in a building and forced to proceed through four tests in succession. In each of the first three tests, he encountered one of the people against whom he sought revenge and that person was in a completely vulnerable state.

Denlon could take his revenge by doing nothing and letting the person suffer and die, or he could forgive and save the person by taking action that would cause Denlon himself to endure some type of physical pain or mental anguish.

Success: Denlon had to complete the first three tests one way or the other within two hours and then he had to complete the final test.

Failure: (1) Denlon would fail to complete the first three tests within two hours, in which case his exit would be sealed and he would be left to die.

(2) Denlon would fail to save any of the first three victims of his tests.

(3) Denlon would fail his final test.

Result: Failure #3

Comments: Kramer wanted to test Denlon's desire for revenge by giving him total power over the lives of the people against whom he sought revenge. Ironically, Denlon did try to save all three, but they died anyway.

1. **Freezer Room**

Movie: *SAW III*

Reason: Danica Scott was the only witness who saw Timothy Young kill Dylan, but she fled the scene and did not testify at trial. If not for her own self-absorption and cowardice, she could have brought Young to justice.

Description: Scott was hanging naked in the middle of a freezer, shackled by her wrists. There were waterspouts on either side of her, which periodically sprayed her with freezing water.

Success: Denlon had to free Scott before she froze to death, which required him to reach between freezing pipes, burning his face in the process, to retrieve the key to Scott's shackles.

Failure: (1) Denlon would do nothing, letting Scott freeze to death.
(2) Denlon would fail to retrieve the key in time to free Scott before she froze to death.

Result: Failure #2

Comments: Denlon found himself face-to-face with the only witness to his son's murder, but now the witness was chained in place and could not escape like she had from the murder scene. Given complete power over Scott's life, Denlon did try to save her, but he let his anger delay his rescue attempt, and this was the cause of his failure.

2. **Pig Vat**

Movie: *SAW III*

Reason: Judge Halden was the judge who presided over Timothy Young's trial. He gave Young a very light sentence.

Description: Halden was chained at the neck to the bottom of a vat. Rotten pig carcasses were being dropped into a nearby meat grinder and the slop created by their ground remains was pouring into the vat. There was an incinerator in the room that was full of Dylan's toys, and a key to Halden's collar was hidden in the toys.

Success: Denlon had to overcome his obsession with Dylan's possessions and turn on the incinerator so that Dylan's toys would be burned and Denlon could then retrieve the key to free Halden.

Failure: (1) Denlon would do nothing, allowing Halden to drown in the slop created by the ground remains of the rotting pigs.

(2) Denlon would fail to unlock Halden's collar in time to prevent the drowning.

Result: Success

Comments: Denlon found himself face-to-face with the Judge who had let his son's killer off with a very light sentence, but now the Judge was to be sentenced by Denlon. Given complete power over Halden's life, Denlon found the strength to save him, even at the expense of losing Dylan's precious possessions.

3. The Rack

Movie: *SAW III*

Reason: Timothy Young killed Dylan in a drunk driving incident.

Description: Young was shackled in a device with collars around his limbs and neck. The collars, in succession, would begin twisting and would eventually completely break Young's arms, legs, and neck. A nearby box contained a key that could free Young. The key was tied to the trigger of a shotgun pointed at the only opening through which a would-be rescuer could insert his arm to retrieve the key.

Success: Denlon had to retrieve the key, likely suffering a shotgun wound in the process, in order to free

Young before the device killed him.

Failure: (1) Denlon would do nothing, allowing Young to be tortured and killed.

(2) Denlon would fail to unlock the device in time to prevent Young from being killed.

Result: Failure #2

Comments: Denlon found himself face-to-face with his son's killer, the confrontation he had obsessed over for so long. Denlon viewed Young as a bearer of death and the cause of his life being ruined, but now Young was presented to him as a vulnerable human being faced with torture and death. In a perfectly Kramer-style twist of fate, Denlon had to decide whether he would take a bullet to save his son's killer. Kramer told Denlon in the instruction tape that he had to decide whether the Golden Rule should apply in this situation. Denlon did retrieve the key, dodging the bullet, but he had agonized about this for a while and it ended up taking too long to free Young. When Denlon dodged the bullet, it ended up killing

Judge Halden, who was standing behind Denlon.

4. Jeff's Final Test

Movie: *SAW III* and *SAW IV*

Set Up: John Kramer

Subject: Jeff Denlon

Reason: Kramer wanted to know if Denlon had learned anything about revenge.

Description: Kramer was on his deathbed with his heart-rate monitor still linked to Dr. Denlon's collar. Next to Kramer's bed was a tray with a host of vicious implements on it. Denlon did not yet know that his daughter, Corbett, had been kidnapped and was being held somewhere by Kramer and his accomplices.

Success: Denlon had to put his obsession with vengeance aside and forgive Kramer for the pain Kramer had caused the Denlons by having them put in traps. This would allow both Jeff and Lynn Denlon to live and would provide them with Corbett's location.

Failure: Denlon would take his revenge, killing Kramer, which would (1) trigger his wife's collar, killing her, (2) prevent Denlon from learning where Corbett was being held, and (3) result in Denlon himself being killed.

Result: Failure

Comments: Kramer wanted to prove that Denlon's rage and vengeance, if pursued, would end up hurting Denlon and his loved ones. Kramer pointed out that taking revenge would only add to Denlon's misery and would neither bring back his son nor allow him to rescue his daughter.

20. The Block of Ice

Movie: *SAW IV*

Set Up: Detective Mark Hoffman; designed by John Kramer

Description: This was an elaborate series of interconnected traps that involved Officer Daniel Rigg (Part A), Kramer's lawyer, Art Blank (Part B), Detective Eric Mathews, and Hoffman himself (Part C).

A. Rigg's Obsession

Subject: Officer Daniel Rigg

Reason: For years, Rigg had witnessed his colleagues die, while he stood by unscathed. Rigg remained unharmed while Mathews had disappeared. However, with Rigg's survival came his obsession—an obsession to stop those around him from making the wrong choices, which prevented Rigg himself from making the right choices. Rigg was so obsessed with saving everyone that he went so far as to take unnecessary risks and act unethically.

Description: Rigg knew that Mathews was still alive because of a video left for him in his apartment, but he did not know Mathews' location. A series of traps were set up to lead Rigg to where Mathews was being held.

Success: Rigg had to learn to overcome his obsession by realizing that the traps were not under his control, that he could not save the test subjects, and that he should just stay at home and pay attention to his loved ones.

Failure: Rigg would try to find Mathews, in which case he would be led through a series of traps that would provide clues to Mathews' location. However, his arrival at Mathews' location would cause Mathews' death.

Result: Failure

Comments: Kramer wanted to test whether Rigg could overcome his obsession, see the world from Kramer's perspective and, in Kramer fashion, give people the opportunity to save themselves.

1. See What I See

Description: A woman named Brenda was sitting in a chair in Rigg's apartment. There were incriminating photographs of Brenda on the walls. Brenda's long hair was pulled back into a ponytail that was ensnared in a device.

Option 1: Rigg would see the clear evidence that Brenda was a prostitute, walk away and leave her in her trap,

which would have allowed Brenda
to be apprehended.

Option 2: Rigg would let his obsession
take over and try to save Brenda,
tripping the device, which would
pull Brenda's ponytail until the
back of her scalp was torn off her
skull, unless he could figure out
how to save her.

Result: Option 2

Comments: In order for Rigg to fully
understand Kramer's message,
he needed to see what Kramer
saw. Rigg needed to see Brenda
not as a victim, but as a criminal
undeserving of the life she leads.

a. <u>Go to Jail</u>

Subject: Brenda

Reason: Brenda was a prostitute.

Description: Brenda assumed that Rigg
would use the photographs on
the wall as evidence of Brenda's
crimes. If Brenda were freed
from the device, which
happened when Rigg figured
out how to stop it, she could
retrieve a nearby knife and
attempt to kill Rigg in order to
escape.

Success: Brenda had to take
responsibility for her crimes

and accept that she would be arrested and probably tried and convicted.

Failure: (1) Brenda would use the knife to kill Rigg and would escape in order to avoid taking responsibility for her crimes.

(2) Brenda would use the knife to try to kill Rigg, but Rigg would kill her in self-defense.

Result: Failure #2

Comments: After killing Brenda, Rigg listened to Brenda's instructional tape and then found a clue to Mathews' location. The clue consisted of two keys together with a card that said, "One saves a life . . . One takes it away."

2. Feel What I Feel

Description: One of the keys Rigg found at the conclusion of See What I See (Part A1) displayed a hotel name, address, and room number. Rigg went to the hotel, which was managed by Ivan Landsness, a serial rapist. Rigg used the key to open the room and was directed to the evidence of Landsness' crimes and the trap that had been set up for Landsness.

Option 1: Rigg would not put Landsness in his trap. If he did this, Rigg would not gain a clue for where to go next, but would gain freedom from his obsession to find Mathews.

Option 2: Rigg would feel appropriate anger toward Landsness and put him in his trap (Part A2a). This would give Rigg a clue to continue his journey, but would also show that he was unable to let go of his obsession.

Result: Option 2

Comments: In order for Rigg to fully understand Kramer's message, he also needed to feel what Kramer felt. Landsness was in desperate need of help and that is why Rigg needed to give Landsness the tools to what Kramer considered to be his salvation, namely his trap. In a way, Landsness' life was in Rigg's hands, but in the end, only Landsness could save himself. Understanding this would put Rigg one step closer to finding Mathews.

a. <u>**Bedroom Trap**</u>

Subject: Ivan Landsness

Reason: Landsness had used his body as an instrument of abuse, committing many acts of rape and other atrocities against women. However, he had been tried of rape only three times and was acquitted each time. As a voyeur, Landsness had kept photographs and videotapes of the many women he had victimized.

Description: Rigg forced Landsness to get on the bed, put restraints on his arms and legs, and put his head in a device with metal spikes above his head pointing at his eyes.

Success: Landsness had to send the metal spikes into both of his eyes, blinding him, but allowing him to remain alive.

Failure: Landsness would be unable to send the metal spikes into his eyes, but they would pierce his eyes anyway and, in addition, all four of his limbs would be ripped from his torso.

Result: Failure

Comments: Kramer wanted to test whether
Landsness could see the pain
he had caused his victims.
Kramer wanted Landsness to
know that he had torn apart
his victims' lives. That is why
Kramer gave Landsness the
opportunity to remain alive
only by sacrificing his eyes, the
instruments that had led him
blindly astray. If Landsness was
unable to make that sacrifice,
then it would be made for him,
and, in addition, the greater
instrument of his crimes, his
body, would be destroyed.
Although this was an extremely
difficult trap to survive, it
seemed fair because the subject
was so evil.

3. <u>Save As I Save</u>

Description: After Rigg forced Landsness into
his trap, Rigg found another clue
that directed him to a school. In
the school, Rigg found a woman
named Morgan and her dead
husband, Rex, suspended back-
to-back in a device. Morgan was
in the process of going through
her own trap (Part A3a), but had
not finished. There was a spike

going through Morgan's arm and also piercing Rex's body. Rigg had the key to free Morgan from the device.

Option 1: Rigg would give Morgan the key and walk away without providing any further help, letting her complete her trap and save herself.

Option 2: Rigg would help Morgan remove the last spike, with the result that Morgan would not have learned to save herself.

Result: Option 2

Comments: In order for Rigg to fully understand Kramer's message, he also needed to save as Kramer saved. To do that, Rigg would need to figure out that Morgan was essentially a student who could be saved only by saving herself. That is why Kramer asked him, "Officer Rigg: Has the pupil learned her lesson?" Upon completion of this trap, Rigg was directed to the room where Mathews was trapped.

a. **Spike Trap**

Subject: Morgan

Reason: Morgan was unable to leave her abusive husband Rex, even though Rex was not only abusing Morgan but also their daughter.

Description: Morgan and Rex were hanging back-to-back in the middle of the room with spikes piercing both their bodies and connecting them. The spikes pierced Morgan's body in locations that could heal if the spikes were removed. The same could not be said for Rex. The spikes pierced his body in locations that would cause fatal bleeding if they were removed.

Success: Morgan had to save herself by pulling the spikes out of her non-fatal wounds, which would also pull the spikes out of Rex's fatal wounds, killing him quickly, but removing the bond between them and allowing her to move forward with her life.

Failure: Morgan would fail to pull the spikes out of the wounds on her body, resulting in both her and Rex bleeding to death slowly.

Result: Success

Comments: In Morgan's instructional tape, Kramer remarked that the human body is a fascinating organism: "It can withstand the most brutal injury and yet repair itself miraculously." This was a reference to Morgan's suffering as well as Kramer's own suffering when he had driven his car off a cliff and somehow miraculously survived. Just as surviving the car crash had empowered Kramer, with this test, Kramer empowered Morgan to take control of her life. Kramer wanted to know whether she could disconnect from the one thing that had brought her and others so much pain.

B. Blank's Final Test

Subject: Art Blank

Description: Blank was keeping watch in the room where Mathews was trapped and Hoffman was pretending to be trapped (Part C). Blank had a device around his neck.

Success: Blank had to perform certain actions in connection with the traps for Rigg and Mathews, such as giving Mathews (Part C) a gun and helping him out of his trap if Rigg passed his test (Part A).

The Cutting Edge

Failure: Blank would fail to perform the required actions and be killed by the device around his neck.

Result: Success—but Blank was killed when Rigg shot him.

C. Mathews' Final Test

Subject: Detective Eric Mathews

Description: Mathews was in a room in Kramer's lair, standing on a block of ice with a noose around his neck. Hoffman appeared to be strapped to a chair that would submerge into a pool of water and electrocute Hoffman if Mathews fell off the ice. Art Blank (Part B) was also in the room, watching Mathews and Hoffman.

Success: Mathews had to remain standing on the block of ice until time expired.

Failure: (1) Mathews would fall off the block of ice and be hanged.
(2) Mathews would give up and hang or otherwise kill himself.

Result: Success—but Mathews was killed because Rigg (Part A) found him and tried to save him.

Comments: This series of tests culminated in one furious scene. Rigg entered the room and shot Blank because he thought Blank was one of Kramer's accomplices. Mathews then shot Rigg because Mathews had been given a gun by Art Blank and assumed that whomever was entering the room was bad. When time expired, two large ice blocks came swinging down to crush Mathews' head. Kramer would have viewed Rigg's death as a just result, because Rigg could not overcome his obsession despite being given numerous opportunities to do so. However, it is difficult to reconcile Blank's and Mathews' deaths because they followed their instructions, but were killed because of Rigg's failure.

21. <u>Your Legacy</u>

Movie: *SAW IV* and *SAW V*

Set Up: Detective Mark Hoffman

Subject: Special Agent Peter Strahm

Reason: Strahm was close to cracking the case and figuring out that Hoffman had become the "new" Jigsaw killer. Hoffman wanted to not only eliminate Strahm, but also to frame him as the new Jigsaw Killer, permitting Hoffman to remain free. Thus, Hoffman said to Strahm, "My legacy will become yours."

Description: Hoffman set up a series of traps for Strahm and his partner, Special Agent Lindsey Perez, who could testify that Strahm was not the new Jigsaw killer.

Result: Unwinnable. Hoffman would continue to set up traps for Strahm until he was killed.

A. <u>Open the Door and You Will Find Me</u>

Movie: *SAW IV*

Subject: Special Agent Peter Strahm

Description: Strahm was led to find the connections between the various parts of Officer Daniel Rigg's trap, which would eventually lead Strahm to the operating room in John Kramer's lair where Kramer had died.

Result: Strahm found Kramer's operating room and body and ended up killing Jeff Denlon.

B. <u>Don't Come Closer</u>

Movie: *SAW IV*

Subject: Special Agent Lindsey Perez

Description: Agent Perez found a doll with an audio recording in it.

Result: When Perez leaned in to try to hear what was being said, the doll's face exploded and the shards pierced Perez's face, sending her to the hospital.

C. <u>The Cube</u>

Movie: *SAW V*

Subject: Special Agent Peter Strahm

Description: Strahm found his way out of the operating room in Kramer's lair and, despite being warned to discontinue his search, continued searching for Hoffman. He was knocked out and when he awoke, his head was in a glass cube that was filling with water.

Result: Strahm performed a tracheotomy on himself in order to continue breathing. Eventually, the police arrived and rescued him.

D. <u>The Coffin</u>

Movie: *SAW V*

Subject: Special Agent Peter Strahm

Description: Agent Strahm was in a room with a glass box that was the size and shape of a coffin. Broken glass covered the bottom of the box.

Result: Strahm was instructed to get in the glass box but he did not. Instead, Hoffman got in the box, which lowered to be level with the floor. The walls of the room then began to close in, crushing and killing Strahm, while Hoffman escaped. Strahm's remains were never found.

22. <u>Real Estate Trap</u>

Movie:	*SAW V*
Set Up:	Detective Mark Hoffman; designed by John Kramer
Reason:	From birth, each of the five test subjects had been given the advantages of few others. Yet, they were unethical and used their advantages only to further themselves at the expense of others. They all made selfish decisions, mostly in terms of their careers. The five subjects conspired to burn down a building and steal the property, which caused the deaths of eight people. All five subjects had escaped blame or punishment for these crimes.
Subjects:	(1) Ashley Kazon
	Specific Reason: Kazon was the fire inspector who wrote a bogus accident report about the incident in order to obscure the truth.
	(2) Charles Saumn
	Specific Reason: Saumn was an investigative tabloid journalist who wrote bogus stories about the incident in order to obscure the truth. He was

also insensitive, cocky, overly aggressive, and cold.

(3) Luba Gibbs

Specific

Reason: Gibbs was a worker in the city planning department who pushed through permits for the building in order to put the plan into action. She had a long history of accepting bribes and cheating people in connection with the issuance of building permits.

(4) Malick Scott

Specific

Reason: Scott was a whiny, panicky junkie. In return for an ounce of heroin from a drug dealer, Scott agreed to burn down the building. Though he believed the building was abandoned, it turned out that there were eight people inside who were killed by the fire Scott set.

(5) Brit Steddison

Specific

Reason: Steddison was a real estate developer who came up with the original idea and set the conspiracy in motion. She knew there were eight people still living in the building, but proceeded with the plan anyway.

Description: The five subjects were in a building. To escape from the building, they had to get through a series of tests.

Success: The five subjects needed to cooperate and work together in order for all of them to survive the tests and escape from the building.

Failure: The subjects would fail to cooperate, leading to the death of one or more of them.

Result: Failure—Kazon, Saumn and Gibbs died.

Comments: Kramer wanted to test just how self-centered each one of these subjects could be. He wanted all five subjects to see that, in order for them to survive, they needed to act as one unit "with the common goal of survival." Kramer told them in the beginning that they were all connected, but he intended this to be double-speak. The group was more likely to interpret this comment to refer to the cable that connected them during their first test. However, in hindsight, the two survivors eventually realized that the real estate scheme was what really connected them.

A. <u>Keys of Life</u>

Description: Each subject wore a neck collar. All five collars were connected via a cable. Mounted on the wall behind each subject was a V-shaped blade capable of decapitation. Across the room from each subject was a pedestal. On top of each pedestal was a glass box containing a key. All five keys were identical; any of them could unlock all five collars. There was no other way to remove the collars. The cable that connected the five collars allowed only one person at a time to retrieve a key, because it pulled everyone else back toward the blades.

Success: The subjects had to realize that any one of the five keys would have unlocked all of the collars on their necks, thus allowing all five to be freed before time expired.

Failure: Each subject would try to retrieve his or her own key, which would not allow enough time for all five to be freed and would result in one or more of them being decapitated.

Result: Failure

Comments: "In choosing how to react to the situation, your lifelong instincts will tell you to do one thing, but I implore you to do the opposite," said Kramer. Kramer was asking them to work together, but because they did not figure this out, Kazon was decapitated.

B. Three Points of Safety

Description: The four survivors were now in a second room. There were glass jars on the ceiling with keys in them. Nail bombs were placed in all four ceiling corners of the room, which would explode when time expired. There were three locked tunnel entrances. Only some of the keys in the glass jars would unlock the doors to the tunnels.

Success: The group had to work together to break the jars, find the keys, unlock the tunnels, and discover that more than one person could fit in each tunnel, so that all of them could safely hide before time expired and the nail bombs exploded.

Failure: Each subject would try to find their own key and hide in their own tunnel, leaving one or more of them to die in the nail bomb explosion.

Result: Failure

Comments: In this trap, Kramer was intentionally misleading with his instructions. "With only three points of safety, which of you will be the odd man out?" he asked. This is misleading because the group was supposed to figure out that they needed to put more than one person in a single tunnel, but the group's instincts, along with the misleading comment from Kramer, resulted in Saumn's death.

C. Close the Circuit

Description: The three survivors were now in a third room. There were five locks on the door and a bathtub filled with water in the center of the room. In order for the group to open the five locks on the door, the electrical circuit powering the door locks needed to be closed. The only way to close the circuit was to connect all five cords to the bath water before time expired.

Success: The group had to work together to discover that each of them could get in the bathtub and suffer a minor shock in order to close the circuit that would open the doors before time expired.

Failure: (1) The group would kill someone and throw their body into the bathrub, to use in order to close the circuit.

(2) The group would fail to work quickly enough, resulting in an electrical current surging through the room and locking the door permanently.

Result: Failure #1

Comments: Kramer again used double-speak in the instructional tape: "The game before you is designed to bridge the gap between you all." This was literally referring to the person they might potentially use to close the circuit, but it was figuratively referring to the gaps they might have bridged if they talked to each other and discovered what they had in common. Their failure resulted in Gibbs' death.

D. <u>Sacrifice of Blood</u>

Description: The two survivors, Scott and Steddison, were now in a fourth room. There was a device that had five holes in it, and in front of each hole was a circular table saw. In the center of the machine was an empty glass beaker. When the beaker was filled to the ten pint mark, the exit door would open.

Success: The group had to realize that each of them could use a saw to slice his or her hand and arm, causing the beaker to fill with their blood and eventually opening the exit door. The greater the number of survivors who made it to this point, the lower the amount of blood each would have been required to "donate" to their common cause.

Failure: (1) The group would force one person to "donate" all ten pints of blood, killing that person.

(2) The group would fail to work together quickly enough, resulting in an electrical current surging through the room and locking the door permanently.

Result: Success

Comments: Kramer finally came forward with his point in this instructional tape. He hoped that their journey had been one of discovery and that they had discovered that "the whole is greater than the sum of its parts." Kramer then goes on to use the human body as an analogy for what he was talking about. He explains: "The human body, for instance, is an astoundingly durable creation. It contains approximately ten pints of blood. Yet it is still able to operate with just half of that." In other words, the human body is capable of doing astounding things when all of its parts are working together correctly. A group of people is capable of the same phenomenon.

23. <u>Pound of Flesh</u>

Movie: *SAW VI*

Set Up: Detective Mark Hoffman; designed by John Kramer

Subjects: Simone and Eddie

Reason: Simone and Eddie lent money to others, knowing they could repossess property worth more than the borrowers could repay. Kramer appropriately called them "predators."

Description: Simone and Eddie were on opposite sides of the room. There was a gated-off section in the middle, which divided the room. A scale was located in the gated-off section. On each side of the gate, there was a hole and a plank on which an object could be pushed through the hole and guided down to one side of the scale. Behind each test subject was a table on which there was a variety of cutting tools. On each subject's head was a piercing device.

Option 1:   Eddie could cut off heavier pieces of his body, tipping the scale to his side and permitting him to escape, in which case the device on Simone's head would pierce her skull and kill her when time expired.

Option 2:   Simone could cut off heavier pieces of her body, tipping the scale to her side and permitting her to escape, in which case the device on Eddie's head would pierce his skull and kill him when time expired.

Result: Option 2—Simone cut off her arm to survive.

Comments: Kramer pointed out to the subjects that the devices on their heads were symbolic of the shackles they placed upon others. Typical of his style, Kramer was turning the tables with this trap, forcing Simone and Eddie into the role of the prey instead of the predator.

24. <u>Mother and Son</u>

Movie: *SAW VI*

Set Up: Detective Mark Hoffman; designed by John Kramer

Subjects: (1) Tara Abbot
               (2) Brent Abbot, Tara's son

Reason: William Easton, a health insurance executive, heartlessly applied his probability formula to deny the claims of Harold Abbot, Tara's husband and Brent's father, effectively condemning Harold to a slow, painful death.

Description: Tara and Brent were in a cage at a zoo. Although they did not know it, they were awaiting the outcome of Easton's Probability Formula trap (Part A). There was a two-way switch in the cage with the labels "Live" and "Die." The switch was next to a container that was full of hydrochloric acid. The container was connected to a device outside the cage.

Option 1:   Tara and Brent could allow Easton to live.

Option 2:   Tara and Brent could condemn Easton to death without knowing how he would die. A device would fall down from the ceiling and pierce Easton's back, injecting him with the hydrochloric acid and melting him from the inside out.

Option 3: Easton could fail his trap and die before reaching Tara and Brent, in which case they would have no decision to make.

Result: Option 2

Comments: Tara and Brent were not guilty of anything. This is why Kramer showed remorse for trapping them and putting them in this situation. Kramer probably thought it was cosmic justice to give Tara and Brent the power over Easton's life. However, Tara and Brent were not made aware of how they would be killing Easton. Perhaps the extreme brutality of Easton's death was somewhat of a punishment for choosing to kill him.

A. <u>Probability Formula</u>

Subject: William Easton

Reason: Easton, one of the top executives at a health insurance company, had a strict probability formula, which he invented, for deciding who was worthy of coverage and who was not. This formula worked to the benefit of healthier patients and to the detriment of sicker patients. It did not take into consideration the will to live, the importance of people to their families, and other difficult-to-quantify human factors. Kramer pointed out in the instruction tape, "When faced with death, who should

live versus who will live are two
entirely separate things."

Description: There were four explosive devices
strapped around Easton's wrists and
ankles, and there were four tests that
he needed to complete.

Success: Easton had to complete the four tests
before time expired, allowing him
to take off the explosive devices and
reach the room where he would await
Tara and Brent's decision.

Failure: Easton would not finish the four tests
before time expired, resulting in
one or more of the explosive devices
detonating and killing him.

Result: Success

Comments: This time, the test was personal. For
the first time, Kramer showed his
face, rather than his puppet's face,
in the instructional video. Of course,
by this time Kramer was already
dead and everybody knew who he
was, so it did not matter anymore.
This implies that Kramer knew he
would be dead by the time this trap
took place. Although he was, in fact,
dead by the time the trap took place,
he said in his instructional tape
to Easton, "You've probably been
wondering when we would see each
other again. Today is that day." These

words were as powerful on tape as
they would have been had Kramer
been there to speak them in person.
In this test, Kramer did not want to
just test Easton; he also wanted to
test Easton's probability formula and
force Easton to apply it to people he
knew.

1. <u>**Oxygen Crusher**</u>

Reason: One of Easton's employees,
Hank, was a 52 year-old, who
continued to smoke despite his
heart condition and high blood
pressure, showing a lack of
appreciation for his own life.

Description: Easton and Hank were both in
separate devices. They had oxygen
masks on their faces, and there
were metal slabs on either side of
their ribcages.

Option 1: Easton could hold his breath
longer than Hank, resulting
in him living and Hank being
crushed by the metal slabs.

Option 2: Easton could allow Hank to hold
his breath longer, resulting in
Hank living and Easton being
crushed by the metal slabs.

Result: Option 1

Comments: Easton had to kill Hank to save
himself. This is exactly what

his probability formula would dictate. However, the harsh reality of directly implementing the formula's result was much more difficult and wrenching than making a cold calculation and sending the result in a letter.

2. <u>**Hanging Trap**</u>

Description: Easton found himself standing in front of two of his employees: Addy and Allen. Addy was Easton's secretary. She was middle-aged and had a family history of diabetes, but was very important to her family. Easton's younger and healthier employee, Allen, did not have any living relatives and was not important to anyone. Addy and Allen were inside a cage, standing on metal ledges with barbed wire nooses around their necks. They were both at risk of hanging in a gruesome manner.

Success: Easton had to save Addy, rejecting his probability formula.

Failure: (1) Easton would save Allen, rigidly applying his probability formula.
(2) Easton would save neither Addy nor Allen.

Result: Success

Comments: According to Easton's probability formula, Addy, being older and weaker, was less worthy of living. However, Easton knew that her loss would be a significant hardship on her family. The younger and healthier Allen could disappear without a blip on the world's radar. It was finally clear to Easton that choosing who should live and who should die is not so easy. Easton was face-to-face with people he knew. Their blood would directly stain his hands. He could no longer apply his formula.

3. <u>Steam Maze</u>

Subject: Easton's lawyer, Debbie

Description: Easton was in a room containing a two-level steam maze. He was on the upper level. Debbie was on the lower level. She had a device locked around her neck. The device was on a timer. If the device was not removed before time expired, it would cause a metal spear to pierce Debbie's brain.

Success: Easton had to help Debbie get through the maze. To do so, he had to let himself get burned several times. He also had to reopen a surgical wound on his stomach to retrieve a key in order to unlock Debbie's device before time expired.

Failure:

(1) Easton would not help Debbie through the maze.

(2) It would take too long to get Debbie through the maze. This would leave insufficient time to retrieve the key and unlock the device.

(3) Debbie would panic and kill Easton in an attempt to get the key.

(4) Debbie would panic and be killed by Easton in self-defense.

Result: Failure #4

Comments: The preceding two traps had shown Easton the flaws in his probability formula. After this trap, he began to understand the extent to which some people will go when faced with death.

4. The Carousel

Reason: Emily, Shelby, Aaron, Dave, Josh and Gena were all employees of Easton. Their findings had resulted in over two-thirds of all applications being denied or prematurely terminated by Easton's company.

Description: The six employees were strapped to a rotating carousel. There was a shotgun nearby that would fire at whomever was in front of it when the carousel stopped. There were two buttons in front of Easton. Pressing one of these buttons would save the person in front of the shotgun while also sending a spike into Easton's hand.

Option 1: Easton could save any two of his six employees by using both buttons.

Option 2: Easton could save any one of his six employees by using one button.

Option 3: Easton could let all six employees die.

Result: Option #1, resulting in Emily and Shelby living and Aaron, Dave, Josh and Gena being shot and killed.

Comments: Kramer wanted to force Easton to apply his probability formula to his own employees. Kramer also wanted to force the employees to feel the consequences of life and death decisions.

25. <u>Reverse Bear Trap II</u>

Movie: *SAW VI*

Set Up: Jill Tuck

Subject: Detective Mark Hoffman

Reason: Hoffman did not value anyone's life but his own. He killed as he pleased. He had the will to survive, but did not understand the value of life.

Description: Tuck set up Hoffman's chair so that it would administer an electric shock when he sat down next. After the shock, Hoffman passed out. Tuck then strapped him into the chair and put the reverse bear trap on his head. This device was hooked into his upper and lower jaws.

Result: Supposedly unwinnable. This trap was designed to be an execution trap. However, Hoffman showed that his will to live was stronger than ever. He broke his thumb in order to slide his hand through the restraint. He used his free hand to get out of the chair restraints. Having no key to unlock the device on his head, he went to the door of the room and bashed the small glass window on it, exposing two metal bars that ran diagonally across the window area. Hoffman put the front of his device in between the two bars, so that when time expired and the device was supposed

to rip open his jaw, it would not be able
to open all the way. The device opened
enough to split open Hoffman's cheek.
He was able to remove the device.

26. <u>Lovers' Triangle</u>

Movie: *SAW: The Final Chapter*

Set Up: Detective Mark Hoffman; designed by John Kramer.

Subjects: (1) Brad
(2) Ryan

Reason: Brad and Ryan's mutual girlfriend, Dina, had lied and manipulated them to the point where they broke the law for her. She played them for fools and caused nothing but pain.

Description: Brad and Ryan were on opposite sides of a table. There were two spinning saw blades on either side of the table. The blades could move from side to side when Ryan or Brad pushed them. Dina hung above the table with a third blade spinning directly below her. The blade under Dina moved as well. This was all publically on display in a shop window.

Success: Both of the spinning saw blades had to stay where they were. Dina would be lowered onto the third blade. This would kill her, but let Brad and Ryan survive.

Failure: (1) Both of the spinning saw blades would be pushed to Brad's side of the table, killing him and letting Dina and Ryan live.
(2) Both of the spinning saw blades would be pushed to Ryan's side of

the table, killing him and letting Dina and Brad live.

Result: Success

Comments: Kramer wanted Brad and Ryan to see that Dina was toxic. Would Brad and Ryan continue to commit crimes for her if the situation was made public? They needed to be strong enough to walk away from what was destroying them. If they could let her go, they would pass the test.

27. <u>Junkyard Trap</u>

Movie: *SAW: The Final Chapter*

Subjects: Officer Matt Gibson and the rest of his police department

Reason: Hoffman wanted to kill Jill Tuck, who was in Gibson's custody.

Option 1:   Gibson would turn Tuck over to Hoffman. Hoffman would kill her, but Gibson would be protecting himself and his colleagues. This would also put a stop to any more traps.

Option 2:   Gibson would protect Tuck. Hoffman would set additional traps designed to kill Gibson, the rest of the police force, and Tuck.

Result: Option 2

A. <u>Glue Seat</u>

Set Up: Detective Mark Hoffman; designed by John Kramer.

Subject: Evan

Reason: Evan and his friends were racist. They had intimidated others based on their physical differences. This was a sufficient reason to test Evan, but Hoffman was also using this trap to attract Gibson and his men to a location where he could kill them.

Description: Evan was sitting in the front seat of a car with his back glued to the car seat. Jacks were holding up the rear of the car. The rear tires were spinning. Evan's girlfriend was tied up below the car. Her head was directly under one of the spinning rear tires. One of Evan's friends was in front of the car. Another friend was chained to the back of the car.

Success: Evan would reach the lever in front of him before time expired. This would save Evan, his girlfriend, and his friends. This would require Evan to rip himself away from the car seat, tearing off the skin on his back.

Failure: Evan would fail to unglue himself before time expired. This would cause the car to fall off the jacks. The car would crush his girlfriend's head, take off, pull off the jaw and arms of the friend who was behind the car, crash into the other friend, and eventually crash into another car, sending Evan flying out the windshield.

Result: Failure

Comments: Evan was told that the situation he found himself in was his own doing. On his instructional tape, he heard, "You've judged others by the color of their skin, and today, Evan, you will learn that we are all the same color on the inside." This was one of Kramer's most clever lines. Though

Kramer designed this trap (his voice is in the instructional tape), it was Hoffman who set up the trap and used to it to ensnare the police.

B. Machine Gun Trap

Set Up: Detective Mark Hoffman

Subjects: Gibson and some other members of his police department.

Reason: Gibson would not hand over Tuck to Hoffman. Hoffman warned Gibson that there would be consequences for this.

Success: The subjects had to determine that the Glue Seat trap (Part A) was a set up to lure them to Hoffman's lair and that they should proceed into the lair with extreme caution or not at all.

Failure: The test subjects would enter the lair with insufficient caution and be killed by a rotating machine gun.

Result: Failure

C. The Cyanide Room

Set Up: Detective Mark Hoffman

Subjects: SWAT Team Members

Reason: Hoffman had promised Officer Gibson that he would kill everyone. While investigating another trap (Trap #28), the SWAT officers came to a room marked "Danger," which they had been warned not to enter.

Success: The SWAT officers had to choose not to enter the room, allowing them to continue searching the building.

Failure: The SWAT officers would enter the room and be trapped inside as the room is filled with deadly gas.

Result: Failure

Comments: Although this trap did not take place at the junkyard, it fit in with the overall trap for the police. Hoffman made sure to kill all of the police so that he could get to Jill Tuck.

28. Liar, Liar

Movie:	*SAW: The Final Chapter*
Set Up:	Detective Mark Hoffman; designed by John Kramer.
Subject:	Bobby Dagen
Reason:	Dagen had written a book about surviving one of Kramer's traps. This book was a hoax. Dagen had never really been in a Jigsaw trap. He deceived his wife, Joyce, who was drawn to him because she believed his story. However, Dagen's lawyer, publicist, and best friend knew the truth and were accomplices in the hoax. Dagen had amassed wealth, fame, and notoriety based on his story of survival.
Success:	Dagen had to proceed through a series of traps in order to free his wife from a cremation device before time expired.
Failure:	Dagen would fail to free his wife before time expired.
Result:	Failure
Comments:	Kramer wanted Dagen's lies to come full circle. He wanted Dagen to truly experience what it would have taken to survive one of his trap. Dagen's wife was an innocent victim used as a tool for punishing Dagen.

A. The Bottomless Cage

Description: Dagen was in a cylindrical metal cage, which was suspended over metal spikes. After the cage was lifted into the air, a lever came down, which Dagen could pull. If the lever were pulled, the bottom of the cage would fall away.

Success: Dagen had to find a way to escape the cage without landing on the spikes.

Failure: Dagen would be impaled on the spikes.

Result: Success

Comments: To Kramer, finding a way out of the cage symbolized the beginning of Dagen's potential rebirth.

B. Speak No Evil

Description: Dagen's publicist, Nina, was strapped in a chair. She had a device around her head and a fishing line going down her throat. The device around her head had four sharp metal spikes pointing toward her neck. This device included a sound meter. The fishing line had a hook at the end with a key attached to it.

Success: Dagen had to save Nina by pulling the fishhook out of her throat and using the key to unlock the device before time expired. In order to do this, both Dagen and Nina had to keep their voices very low to avoid tripping the sound meter.

Failure: (1) Dagen could take too long to pull the key out and Nina's throat would be pierced by the metal spikes.

                (2) Dagen and/or Nina could speak too loudly during the process of pulling out the key, causing the metal spikes to pierce Nina's throat.

Result: Failure #1 and #2

Comments: Nina had been Dagen's publicist for years, knowing his lies, but choosing to "speak no evil." She had been richly rewarded for her false publicity, but in her trap, she would have been rewarded only for her silence. In the end, she proved incapable of remaining quiet, even in a life or death situation.

C. See No Evil

Description: Dagen's lawyer, Suzanne, was strapped in front of a device that could send three sharp metal spikes into her eyes and mouth. A weight was attached to the device.

Success: Dagen had to save Suzanne by lifting the weight to its highest setting. This would send metal spikes into his sides, but would also stop the device from piercing Suzanne's face.

Failure: Dagen would not hold the bar up high or long enough. This would cause the metal spikes to pierce Suzanne's face, killing her.

Result: Failure

Comments: This was the price Suzanne had to pay for pretending to "see no evil."

D. Hear No Evil

Description: Dagen and his best friend, Cale, were on opposite sides of the room. The floor between them was missing and a small path was constructed of plywood. Cale had a noose around his neck and could not see because he was blindfolded.

Success: Dagen had to save Cale by directing him to walk in the correct direction and remain on the plywood path. This could allow Cale to reach Dagen and receive the key that would unlock his device before time expired.

Failure: (1) Cale would fall off the plywood boards and be hanged.
(2) The key would be dropped.
(3) Cale would not get the key in time.

Result: Failure #2

Comments: Cale knew of Dagen's sins, yet acted as though he heard no evil. On that day, what he heard was the difference between life and death.

E. <u>Pulling Teeth</u>

Description: Dagen was in a small room. There was a lock on the door to the next room where his wife, Joyce, was held captive. The combination to the lock was etched on his top back molars.

Success: Dagen had to pull out his top back molars to look at the numbers etched on them and then enter the combination in the lock, open the door, and gain access to the room where Joyce was held captive.

Failure: Dagen would not be able to open the door before time expired, in which case Joyce would be killed.

Result: Success

F. <u>Meat Hook Trap</u>

Description: Dagen was separated from Joyce by an electric fence. In front of him were two meat hooks hanging on metal chains. At the top of the chains was a disconnected electrical cable. This was a replication of the fictional trap Dagen had claimed to survive.

Success: Dagen had to realize that the trap he claimed to survive was impossible to survive and find another way to connect the cable to save Joyce.

Failure: Dagen would try to solve the trap in the way he claimed he had. He would pierce the meat hooks through his pectoral muscles and try to hoist himself up to the electric cable. This would result in the hooks breaking through his pectoral muscles because they could not support his weight. Dagen would fall to the ground with too little time left to figure out another way to save Joyce.

Result: Failure

Comments: Kramer told Dagen that his final task would be the most difficult. Kramer's instructions mimicked Dagen's fictitious escape, but Dagen had to figure out that he could not pass the test that way. Upon failing, Dagen was left alive, yet all of the people he was supposed to have saved were dead. Dagen is the only person to have completely failed a test and still remain alive. We have no information on what happened to him afterwards.

29. <u>Reverse Bear Trap III</u>

Movie: *SAW: The Final Chapter*

Set Up: Detective Mark Hoffman

Subject: Jill Tuck

Reason: Tuck had tried to kill Hoffman.

Description: Hoffman strapped Tuck into a chair and placed the reverse bear trap on her head.

Result: Unwinnable. Even if Tuck had managed to escape the device itself, Hoffman would have been there to kill her.

30. <u>Bathroom Trap III</u>

Movie: *SAW: The Final Chapter*

Set Up: Dr. Lawrence Gordon

Subject: Detective Mark Hoffman

Reason: Hoffman murdered Jill Tuck and many others.

Description: Gordon shackled Hoffman's ankle to a pipe and permanently locked him in the same decrepit bathroom where Gordon and others had been trapped (Trap #10 and Trap #15).

Result: Unwinnable. There was no way for Hoffman to escape. In an homage to John Kramer, Gordon said "game over" as he closed and sealed the bathroom door.

Trap of Unknown Time

Lawnmower Trap

Movie:	*SAW: The Final Chapter*
Set Up:	Unknown
Subjects:	(1) Sidney
	(2) Alex
Reason:	Sidney felt incapable of breaking away from her abusive boyfriend, Alex.
Description:	Sidney and Alex were hanging onto ladders above upturned lawnmowers.
Option 1:	Alex could knock Sidney off the ladder, sending her down into the lawnmower blades below them.
Option 2:	Sidney could knock Alex off the ladder, sending him down into the lawnmower blades below them.
Result:	Option 2
Comments:	This trap was revealed in a flashback by a member of the support group established by Bobby Dagen for survivors of Jigsaw traps.

ACKNOWLEDGMENTS

There are many people who helped me with this project, and I am very grateful to all of them even though I can mention only a few. First, I could not have done this without my dad. He initially thought this project lacked merit, but that would never stop him from helping, and after he read the second draft of my senior philosophy thesis, he was a believer. Writing this book has brought us closer together, which further fueled my work, and dad spent many rigorous hours and all-nighters helping me edit, sometimes sending his comments to me at 5-o'clock in the morning only for me to return my next draft 24 hours later. We watched the movies together, discussing the philosophical connotations and importance of various scenes. I will never be able to thank him enough for all the help he has given me on this project.

Second, I must thank my mom, who detests gory horror movies, but was able to put that aside in order to not only help me sort out my thoughts on the *SAW* series, but to also watch the movies with me (although she did have to cover her eyes often). During the emotional struggle that I had while watching each *SAW* film about twenty times, my mom's support gave me the strength to keep researching.

Third, my fiancé has been a great inspiration to me. It is because of this book that we first met; he attended a discussion and celebration of my senior philosophy thesis. Since then, his unwavering support has helped me believe in myself and persist with this project long enough to turn it into a book.

Fourth, my sister and brother-in-law were key early supporters. They provided valuable insights into some of the hidden plot twists and helped me crystallize my thoughts on the movies.

Fifth, I'd like to thank my college philosophy department for its guidance, access to books, and education in many aspects of philosophy. Once I had the original ideas scoped out, it was my college philosophy classes that gave me the ability to look at *SAW* in a scholarly light.

Last but not least, one of the greatest inspirations to my writing is my high school English teacher, who taught me most of what I know about writing. Though it has been seven years since I have had class with him, his lessons still ring in my head every time I write.

Printed in Great Britain
by Amazon